Frank Wedekind

SPRING'S AWAKENING

Tragedy of Childhood

Library of Congress Cataloging-in-Publication Data

Library of Congress Card Number: 96-85180

British Library Cataloging-in-Publication Data

A catalog record of this book is available from the British Library.

Applause Theatre & Cinema Books
19 West 21st Street, Suite 201
New York, NY 10010
Phone: (212) 575-9265
Fax: (212) 575-9270
Email: info@applausepub.com
Internet: www.applausepub.com

Applause books are available through your local bookstore, or you may order at www.applausepub.com or call Music Dispatch at 800-637-2852

Sales & Distribution:
North America:
    Hal Leonard Corp.
    7777 West Bluemound Road
    P.O. Box 13819
    Milwaukee, WI 53213
    Phone: (414) 774-3630
    Fax: (414) 774-3259
    Email: halinfo@halleonard.com
    Internet: www.halleonard.com

Frank Wedekind

SPRING'S AWAKENING

Tragedy of Childhood

English version and Ten Notes by
Eric Bentley

APPLAUSE
NEW YORK • LONDON

A DEDICATION

Wedekind dedicated his play to the Man in the Mask, who is a character IN the play, and one which Wedekind himself sometimes played. Was it himself? Was it life? Was it Goethe? In any event, more than a hundred years have passed, and here is another edition, another version. If there is a Man in a Mask, it is the present publisher, hiding behind the words "Applause Theatre Books": my friend, Glenn Young. I must, and happily do, dedicate this new version of the play to him.

E.B.

CONTENTS

Ten Notes

FOOTPRINTS IN THE SANDS OF TIME

1891   Spring's Awakening published at the author's expense in Zurich.

1906   Max Reinhardt directs the world première in Berlin.

1909   Published in the U.S. in a translation by Francis J. Ziegler.

1912   First production in the U.S. In German: at the Irving Place Theatre, New York. In a brief, anonymous review, *The New York Times* declares the play would not be popular in America because (a) of its subject matter and (b) of its "lax construction" in fifteen [sic] scenes.

1917   First American production in English: a single matinée at the Thirty-Ninth Street Theatre, New York. Producer: The Medical Review of Reviews. Slightly before curtain time, the City Commissioner of Licenses arrives and states that the play cannot be performed, but an injunction from a Supreme Court [of New York] judge allows the curtain to go up around four. *The New York Times:* "With many sniggers, rollings of the eye, and gestures indicating intellectual freedom, a large and strangely compounded audience assembled yesterday afternoon . . . to witness *Frühlingserwachen* at its first performance in what you might call English . . . Present were Emma Goldman, Geraldine Farrar, and Elizabeth Marbury, who withdrew as soon as possible . . . There was an elderly gentleman who whiled away the intervals between acts reading *The Birth Control Review.*"

1918–   Wedekind dies. World War I ends, and with it the cen-
1933   sorship of the old regime in Germany and Austria-

Hungary. During the Weimar Republic, 1918-1933, the play is freely produced. A 1929 production in Berlin with Peter Lorre and Lotte Lenya in the cast gains considerable notoriety.

1933- Not being either Jewish or Communist, Wedekind is not
1945   officially proscribed. His official biographer Artur Kutscher, himself a Nazi, is at pains to explain to the government how pure was Wedekind's Aryan blood. But he hadn't written the kind of thing the Nazis wanted produced, so they didn't produce him: a story that would later be told by his widow, Tilly, in her memoir, *Lulu: Rolle Meines Lebens*.

1958   In consultation with Wedekind's daughter, Kadidja, Eric Bentley prepares a translation for production by the University of Chicago Theatre.

ERECTIONS AND EJACULATIONS

In the second half of the 19th century, literature opened up the actualities of sex as never before, and great "innovative" artists such as Baudelaire, Flaubert, and Zola were all in trouble with the law over their alleged indecency. Especially the eighties and nineties were a time of sexual revolution. One can place most of the revolutionary literature between parentheses marked by Krafft-Ebing's *Psychopathia Sexualis* in 1886 and Freud's *Interpretation of Dreams* in 1900. Havelock Ellis' multi-volume *Psychology of Sex*, coming out serially during this period, made "sexology" a subject for a wide stratum of the public.

The "dirty play" of the early nineties, in England, at least, was Ibsen's *Ghosts*, and Strindberg plays such as *The Father* and *Miss Julie* were beginning to be seen in the capitals of the West. The theatre critics were duly shocked, but the sex in theatre was understandably far less explicit than it had already been in novels such as Zola's *Nana* or the stories of Maupassant. Bernard Shaw's *Mrs. Warren's Profession* was banned in England for decades, but it contained no raunchy or even blunt language—Mrs. Warren's *profession* is never named—and it displays no nude or even semi-nude bodies or love-making.

So plays like *Ghosts* were able to reach a theatre audience and shock it, while *Spring's Awakening* was not allowed to reach theatres lest Western civilization go up in smoke. When Wedekind finally found a publisher for the play, the latter refused to go ahead unless the author paid the whole bill. Performances did not come for fifteen years after that, and only in a heavily cut text. Wedekind was so "explicit" in this play that he seemed to many of his readers closer to the underground erotica of the Victorian age (which abounded) than to any dramatic literature aboveground. His play asked the impossible of the Victorian theatre: that it exhibit on stage the sexuality of thirteen- and fourteen-year-old boys. (He did not go so far as to ask for equal can-dor about girls.)

How explicit is "explicit"? In the 1990s, XXX "adult" movies are on display in all big American cities and are marketed for screening in hotels and private homes in millions of video cas-settes. Live theatre, even today, could not be as "explicit" as these films are, if only because actors cannot get erections and ejacu-lations on cue, but Wedekind was the first dramatist to intro-duce the subject of erections and ejaculations. At certain points in the action of *Spring's Awakening* we are meant to believe they are actually happening, though one takes for granted that they are not meant to be actually seen. Masturbation hovers over the whole play, and is announced to be taking place on stage in Act III, Scene 4, but there again one would not expect to see it. (Most stage directors haven't even realized that that is what is going on. Those who have placed the actors with their backs to the audience, as was done in the Broadway musical *Oh! Calcutta!* [1969] in similar circumstances.) What is often called "The Masturbation Scene" (Act II, Scene 3) actually shows a boy pushing away the temptation to masturbate. Among sexual acts, only the rape of Wendla is fully there, on stage and facing front, and, of course, it has to be faked—the politer word is *acted*.

So: Was Wedekind explicit? No, if you are thinking in terms of XXX movies. Yes, if your mind is on the issues. And in this play, not only are teenage pregnancy and abortion big issues, "stirrings of manhood" are very much an issue—one that helps drive Moritz Stiefel to suicide. He has been so amazed at his first erections, so terrified by his first ejaculations.

There is more to say about the enacted rape. If an audience thinks it is seeing actual intercourse on stage—or something very close to it—they will not be able to think of anything but the shock they are receiving (or the surprise or whatever), but, knowing full well that the act is only simulated, they are free to recognize the complexity of the episode. It is not just a matter, as all the censors thought, of a girl being "had" by a boy. It is a matter of the particular attitudes to these two: Wendla, who is saying, "Don't love me, because it's love that makes a girl pregnant!" and Melchior, who is not denying this proposition, but explaining that he doesn't love her because love doesn't exist. Wedekind is not dramatizing juvenile sex as such, but is bringing together two young people, each of whom has just arrived at a certain view of things: Wendla at her mother's (pretended) view of childbirth, Melchior at adolescent rebelliousness and unbelief. And, at their previous meeting, the incipient masochism in Wendla has brought out the hitherto unconscious sadism in Melchior which now, in the hayloft, bursts into flame.

CENSORSHIP

Spring's Awakening has been one of the most censored of all plays. When it was not banned altogether, many passages and words were changed or deleted. It would be hard to gather all the evidence because Germany did not have a single national censorship but censored differently in each locality. Here are some doubtless typical facts from Erhard Weidl's notes in a recent German edition:

• Among the words (here translated) ordered to be replaced were: Priapia (where Priapus reigns), copulation, abortion pills, stirrings of manhood.

• Three scenes were cut in their entirety, namely, the scene of Hänschen Rilow refraining from masturbation (Act II, Scene 3), the Reformatory scene in which the inmates do masturbate (Act III, Scene 4), and the vineyard scene in which Ernst kisses Hänschen (Act III, Scene 6).

• The language of the youngsters was much doctored. For example, (in I.2) Melchior was not allowed to ask Moritz if he had ever seen two dogs running together across the street. The following formulation was substituted: "Have you ever seen how, for example—in a certain way—if I can put it this way—."

• In Prague (Austria-Hungary), the following conditions were attached to the performance of the key scene in the hayloft where Wendla becomes pregnant: "Only a concealed presentation is permitted. The stage is to be darkened as much as possible. Melchior and Wendla must not lie on top of each other but sit side by side with a space between them."

• Trying to help things along under the restricted circumstances, Wedekind wrote a stage direction for an acting edition in which he proposed that the darkness of the hayloft scene be punctuated by flashes of lightning while thunder, roaring throughout, is punctuated by a few loud bangs.

Although these horrid examples are German (or Austro-Hungarian), they have a bearing elsewhere and even after 1918. My own translation of *Spring's Awakening*, which dates from 1958, bore the marks of a German acting edition which, all unknown to me, was bowdlerized. For example, where Wedekind had written that Wendla's sister had had three children in two years of marriage, thus informing us that she had been pregnant before the wedding, my translation gives the figure as two and a half years, thus rendering Ina respectable. A small point, but typical. A larger point has to be made about Emma Goldman's citations of the play in a lecture she gave in 1914, later a chapter in her book *The Social Significance of Modern Drama*. It is clear from Emma Goldman's account that she used a text that suppressed a key event in the story: that Wendla was killed by abortion pills. She thinks, apparently, that Wendla was too fragile to bring a child to birth, whereas Wedekind, in the full text, tells us, via the Masked Man, that she was physically strong and would have lived to have a healthy child.[1]

Again, though it is impossible to collect all the facts, it is clear that, even when uncut texts were available both in German and in translation, theatres continued to exercise a censorship of their own. When my own earlier translation was first performed—in the late fifties and early sixties—I was a witness to the way directors, sometimes without omitting or changing any dialogue, can keep the audience from noticing what is going on. Thus, for example, in the vineyard scene (Act III, Scene 6), where a boy should kiss another boy, thus openly showing his feelings, an actor, in a production I saw, simply shared his cigarette with

---

1 Even in the Applause reprint of her book (1987), Emma Goldman is allowed, without editorial comment, to say that *Spring's Awakening* has fourteen scenes, whereas in fact it has nineteen. The first American production (1912), according to *The New York Times*, had fifteen scenes. One must assume that early American accounts are based on abridged versions which wreck the structure of the play as well as leaving holes in the narrative.

his partner, a gesture which incidentally made the characters seem much older than kissing would have.

The characters seemed much older? On stage, ever since the world premiere in 1906, the characters in *Spring's Awakening* have always seemed older than they should have. The youngsters are thirteen or fourteen. So far as I know, they have always been played by grownups, even grownups, in many cases, well over twenty-five. Small productions in the U.S. have used college students, sometimes as young as eighteen. But, in *Spring's Awakening*, there is just as crucial a difference between fourteen and eighteen as there would be between fourteen and ten. The eighteen-year-olds are young men—*ephebes*—if male; if female, young wives and the like. To cast *Spring's Awakening* with these older people is to continue to censor it and thereby render it bland and innocuous, and to miss Wedekind's whole point. Spring has gone back to sleep as summer beckons.

MORITAT

What story does *Spring's Awakening* tell? Introducing *The First Lulu* in my edition of that play, I turned its story into a Moritat — one of those metrical tales of mayhem in which Central Europeans used to get their daily or weekly news on the street. In form, Wedekind's early plays seem derived from Moritaten, though, literally, they are not. But my main motive for using a Moritat in both these cases is that censors, critics, and stage directors have conspired to distract us from what Wedekind was actually relating. The Moritat points the index finger at each incident – and this pointing at the "visual aids" to singing which he brought with him in the form of illustrations — blow-ups of comic books, if you will.

Spring's Awakening

(There are various old tunes that would fit these words since the meter, in the language of hymn books, is 8.7.8.7. Kurt Weill composed his *Mack the Knife* in this meter, and William Bolcom has written a new tune for the following, as also for the Lulu Moritat.)

Here's a mini-Reign-of-Terror
War uncivil to the knife
Which beset three little people
In the springtime of their life.

See these children in the schoolyard
Of an ancient German town!
Watch their games and hear their voices!
And observe what shot them down.

Hark to Melchior and Moritz
And to Wendla, Melchi's friend.
Two of them knew springtime's pleasures.
Two met with a frightful end.

Melchi's fourteen, Wendla's thirteen.
Winter now his exit makes.
They're together in a hayloft.
Thunderclap! The Spring awakes!

When she *said* No, did she mean it?
Melchi did not say she lied
And when, later, people asked him:
Was it rape? Yes, he replied.

And the tryst had consequences.
Wendla did not feel quite well.
Ma, who recognized the symptoms,
Thought her daughter bound for hell.

How keep her from Satan's clutches?
Save her from th'infernal pit?
Ma admitted she was flummoxed
Then remembered: Mother Schmidt.

Smitty is the local midwife:
In your home or in her room
She can bring to birth a baby
Or destroy it in the womb.

And when people tell Old Smitty
Baby is a child of sin
She provides the Smitty Tablets
That will do the infant in.

And sometimes the Smitty Tablets
Do more than they're asked to do.
Killing little Wendla's offspring
They took care of Wendla too.

On a charge of rape and rapine
Melchior now went to jail
While his classmate Moritz Stiefel
—Hear it, folks, and weep! Turn pale!

For the timid, wide-eyed Moritz
Spring's awakening was grim
No threat to the girls like Melchi
Girls, he felt, were threatening *him*.

For while Melchi had fared onward
In *his* spring's awakening

Moritz had fared ever inward
Into dire imagining.

Life's too much! He cannot take it!
What he does take is a gun.
Sticks the barrel 'twixt his teeth and
Blows his head up at the sun.

Where stands Melchi now? O horror!
Both his friends have died on him.
"Sink or swim?" That is the question.
He prepares to sink, not swim.

And now something spooky happened:
Melchior to the graveyard came.
First thing that he saw — you guessed it —
On a headstone: WENDLA'S NAME —

Near the stone, the ghost of Moritz,
Underneath his arm, his head.
And near Moritz, a MASKED STRANGER
Screams as if to wake the dead:

MELCHI, DO NOT FOLLOW MORITZ!
COME BACK FROM THAT DREADFUL BRINK!
SINK OR SWIM? Dive in and swim, lad,
Swim so that you CANNOT sink!

Moritz and the STRANGER vanish.
Wendla's corpse will ne'er grow warm.
Melchi meets the STRANGER's challenge
And strides out into the storm.

MORAL

When your daughter is eleven
— On her body signs of spring —

Let her (if she'd get to heaven)
Study SPRING'S AWAKENING.

OTHER NEWS

Not all whom the spring awakened
Killed themselves or broke the law.
Hansi bought some picture postcards,
Lovely ladies in the raw:

And he dreamed he was Othello
Murd'ring Desdemona sweet
As he flushed the naked ladies
Down below his toilet seat—

Thus did Hans remove temptation,
But, returning to his class,
Noticed that his classmate Ernest
Had a photogenic ass.

"May I take your picture, Ernest?
In the nude would be just fine!"
Rolling in the grass together
They invented sixty-nine.

BLOOD BROTHERHOOD

In the Moritat, we see the action of *Spring's Awakening* through the eyes of a street journalist. He sensationalizes, and that involves a certain amount of distortion. Thus, where, in the play, Wendla is fourteen as of Scene 1, this precursor of supermarket tabloids makes her thirteen. Such a journalist's sins of omission are even greater. He underplays the non-sexual friendship of Melchior and Moritz in order to concentrate the more on the Wendla story. He is cruder than Wedekind in portraying the gay relationship of Hänschen and Ernst. And so on. In short, the Moritat does not replace the play, or come near covering all the ground. Time, then, to attempt to cover it in another way—first, by looking into origins. The origin is not the essence but it can help us see a process and an emergence: not what a thing is, but what it comes to be.

Spring's Awakening came out in 1891. Twenty years after that event, Wedekind looked back:

> I began writing without any plan, intending to write what gave me pleasure. The plan came into being after the third scene and consisted of my own experiences or those of my schoolfellows. Almost every scene corresponds to an actual incident ...

There would be little point in working out a demonstration of this matching of art and real life, page by page, but Wedekind's schoolboy letters help us discover the state of mind from which his play gradually emerged, and one account by another hand brings a central matter of his play into sharp focus.

Among the boys of Aarau, Switzerland, where Wedekind went to school in the seventies and early eighties, there occurred a veritable wave of suicides. In 1880 two boys named Rotner and Ruetschi shot each other to death. Sophie Haemmerli-Marti (1866–1942), a poet of the Aarau dialect and a friend of the young Wedekind, reports how he and his dear friend Schibler

accidentally happened to meet on the scene of this bloody event
shortly after it happened.

> On the way home, one night, from the "Kreuz" [a tavern?],
> these two…landed on a bench by the suspension bridge where
> the two boys had just been found and carried off. They had not
> been able to come to terms with their sufferings and had found
> no other way out than to shoot each other. Franklin [Wedekind]
> was utterly devastated. He knelt by the bench, dipped his hand-
> kerchief in the blood, and wanted to die on the spot. Schibler
> talked to him for two hours in that dark valley till he finally
> came to himself. But next morning, day had scarcely dawned
> when all hell broke loose again. They wept buckets and Franklin
> implored his friend on his knees to please lend him his father's
> pistol. After much to and fro they finally came to the conclusion
> that they should start a new life in memory of the two dead boys
> and swear blood brotherhood for ever and ever. Gingerly, gin-
> gerly each stabbed the other in the arm with a pen knife and let
> a drop of blood run into the Burgundy which they had stolen
> from the cellar and now drank up to the dregs, their arms inter-
> locked.

Publishers and publicists have dubbed Wedekind's plays
Tragedies of Sex, and therefore, like our street minstrel, they have
seen *Spring's Awakening* as principally the story of Melchior and
Wendla. That it is the story of Melchior has been clear, of course,
to everyone, and even the most casual reader or spectator has been
able to say, "Melchior must be Wedekind, the play is, in the first
instance, a portrait of the artist as a young…boy." If it is also the
story of Wendla, it is no less the story of a third character: Moritz
Stiefel. The richness of the drama derives in no small part from this
duality — Melchior/Wendla, Melchior/Moritz. Interesting about
the account provided to us by the Aarau poet is that the Wendla
theme is entirely absent. Wedekind, there, is a boy among boys.

Interesting, too, is that no reason is given for the suicides. It's
an epidemic. People are killing themselves because other people

have already killed themselves. Wedekind is prescribing precisely this remedy for himself: tormented by the death of schoolfellows, he wishes to contribute his own death, and apparently *would* so contribute it, were it not for – what? A friend talks him out of it in the name of Blood Brotherhood, ancient Teutonic jargon for what modern jargon calls Male Bonding. Interesting, again, is that this scene from "real life" is more openly, gushingly emotional than any scene in *Spring's Awakening*. Some of this emotion is recaptured in the play but recollected, if not in tranquility, at least in a certain wry detachment: what might have led to tragedy, or pure pathos, is tragi-comedy, shot though with irony, and not without outright humor. One would never have been able to deduce the story the Aarau poet tells from the play Wedekind wrote. Yet much of her story is *in* the play — less in the facts, perhaps, than in the aura — the sense of a particular human cosmos.

GOD THE FATHER, FATHER THE GOD

The death of God proclaimed by Nietzsche in the 1880s was the death of the father principle. A revolt against paternal authority was perhaps the greatest of the several great upheavals of those days. Its great document in English literature—published only later precisely because of its excessively explosive character—was Samuel Butler's *Way of All Flesh.* In German literature it had many documents, one of which has particular interest here: *Das Friedensfest, a "Family Catastrophe in Three Acts,"* by Gerhart Hauptmann. It antedates *Spring's Awakening* by one year, and happens, though not overtly, to be about Frank Wedekind and his father.

The teenage Wedekind found himself aligned with his Mother in a war against his Father. The war culminated and ended in the son actually striking the father, at which point Frank left home, assuming his father would never forgive him. The assumption proved to be mistaken but the trauma had lasting repercussions—the play *Spring's Awakening* surely being one. If this is not immediately obvious, it is because Wedekind abhorred the "naturalistic" obviousness of, for example, Hauptmann's presentation, and preferred to set "real life" material at a remove—"alienating" it in a manner that would later be called Brechtian.

But it is known that the tone of the dialogue in the big scene (Act III, Scene 3) between Mr. and Mrs. Gabor is the characteristic tone of Wedekind's parents. Dramaturgically, formally, the scene may be modeled, as Wedekind says, on the Dismal Day scene in *Faust I,* but its substance is a depiction of the Victorian father and the Victorian mother written by a son who resented the former and pitied the latter. Measured in lines, Mr. Gabor does not have a big role in the play: He is only in this one scene.

But this scene happens to be the keystone in the house that Frank built.

The conventionally well-made plays of the period are integrated in the French manner: they rise to a single climax, all other episodes properly subordinated. Wedekind adopted the structure which Brecht later would call epic, and which was inherited from the Elizabethans via Goethe: it aims not at a single luminous image, but at varied perspectives. What is the main scene, the *scène à faire*, in a play like *Spring's Awakening*? Viewed from one vantage point, it is the hayloft scene, on which so much hinges. From another, it is the final scene—because so much culminates there, and in which a final reversal is effected. Another factor is thematic interaction, and I am citing the final scene here because it picks up the paternity theme from the earlier scene of the Gabor parents—in which already much had culminated, and a decisive reversal had been effected. As to these reversals: in the earlier scene, the actual Father turns the Mother around with the result that Melchior is propelled toward death. In the later scene, Melchior is turned back toward life by a figure he at first takes to be his Father but who is actually . . . well, who? The details must be looked at.

"Are you my father?" Melchior asks the Man in the Mask. On its face, the question is gratuitous. It makes sense only as coming from very deep inside Melchior. In the haunt of death— where lies Wendla's corpse and where he has already encountered the ghost of a headless Moritz—there suddenly appears an older male figure. Melchior's father's minions are on his trail. Could it be that his father—no ghost but the flesh and blood reality—has tracked him down, now, to this place which bids fair to be his deathbed? Wendla had brought death. Moritz had brought death. Would his father now end the long tyranny of paternity by actually killing him? It would be a direct inversion of the parricide theme as it lurked in the Wedekind home and in Gerhart Hauptmann's account thereof.

The Masked Man answers, in effect, "My face may be hidden but wouldn't you recognize your own father's voice?" To which Melchior retorts that he would not. He would not recognise the voice of his own father? Astonishing. Seeing an older man, the first thing he thinks of is his father. Yet in no time at all he has forgotten his father's voice! His father is now ever-present but infinitely distant.

Who *is* the Masked Man? Where Gerhart Hauptmann would have offered a single and right answer, the Wedekindian dramaturgy does not: it even ends up suggesting this may not be the right question. Not that definite answers are absent. One is given to Moritz: the man is Life itself, offset by Death. A "quote" from Goethe suggests that Goethe himself may be on stage. The way the play is written, plus the fact that Wedekind sometimes played this part, have led some to suppose that the Man is none other than the Author. Characters have been "in search of an author" and have found him!

Melchior asks him to announce that he is A or B or C. That is natural, but the Man is not a natural phenomenon. One German stage director took it that most of the final scene is a dream of Melchior's. That is stretching a point, yet in inviting us to define the Man *through Melchior* it is helpful. Note this exchange:

> MELCHIOR: Who are you? I can't entrust myself to a man I don't know.
> MAN: You can't get to know me unless you entrust yourself to me.

This is a quasi-religious proposition, akin to "Whosoever willeth to do His will shall know of the teaching, where it be of God." So perhaps the Man *is* Melchior's father? Or God the Father? It depends on Melchior. Can he give his trust? At puberty, he has come to mistrust everyone and everything, has lost his faith in God the Father and more particularly in Father the God. The former's presence had never been certain, but the latter was a flesh and blood reality. Now that Melchior and his Father have rejected each other, what is the boy's image of the source of his being? It is the image of an evil Giant. While the Father comes to see the son as Wicked, Perverse, and Criminal, the son, in equal measure, demonizes the father.

Now the Man, in talking realistically about the Father, does not rehabilitate him, he deflates him, reduces him to manageable size. While Melchior is still seeing images of an angry Yahweh, the Man remarks, "Your father at the moment is seeking solace in the doughty arms of your mother." Sexual intercourse—center of the universe of this play—the thing that Melchior was in so much trouble for doing is what Papa is indulging in as a soothing sequel to the big scene on his high moral horse! Here at last Wedekind makes sex (which his play represents as the legitimate pursuit of teenagers) disgusting. The sex Melchior has indulged in was not beautiful, it was violent and anguished, but it was not, like the sex his father now "enjoys," banal and distasteful: it was not ridiculous.

How, by the way, does the Man know what Melchior's parents are up to? If he's a dream figure, you may retort, anything is possible, but in such scenes of Wedekind, naturalistic explanations, though they don't tell the whole truth, contribute, and there is one person present who, if he couldn't know, could guess. This is Melchior, and at this point we realize that, on one plane, the Man is part of Melchior, a part to be sure that Melchior has hitherto chosen to ignore. It is the father within. The Man is offering to be a new father, a father within, if only Melchior will trust him, i.e., for the first time, trust himself. The Man is not the father that begat him, but the father he now begets—through intercourse with himself.

Intercourse with oneself! As the song had it, in the musical *Hair*, masturbation can be fun. It can even transcend itself and become an acceptance and celebration of the self—body and soul.

MORITZ/MELCHIOR:
KEITH/SCHOLZ ET AL.

Moritz is to be condemned—by Melchior and by us, the audience—not so much, however, because he "is" death, as because, finally, of the terms on which he accepts death. He claims to be able to offer Melchior a transcendence of defeat through a particular stance: namely of being, in death, serenely superior to those who are still living, smiling at the mere futility that is human life. Melchior has not adopted this stance even at the point where he is still considering suicide. He is in despair, but he had not accepted any rationale that might legitimize despair, let alone make him smile. It is here that the Man in the Mask cuts in. Just as Melchior has "mystified" his father, who must be promptly demystified, so Moritz has "mystified" *his* parents. He had thought that, if he flunked out at school, his parents wouldn't have been able to take it. "I took up the murderous weapon for my parents' sake." To which the Man responds:

> Don't kid yourself, my friend. Your parents would no more have died of it than you need have. Strictly considered, they would have raged and thundered only from physical need.

Notable, now, about Moritz is that, first, the Man is right, and his own philosophy of being above the battle is phony and that, second, he nonetheless reverts to that philosophy when left to himself, and Wedekind chooses to end the play with a reassertion, by Moritz, of the philosophy just exposed as phony. Is that comedy? It is not tragedy. It is Wedekindian tragi-comedy. It is appropriate, somehow, that this at all points dual and dialectical drama not end straightforwardly "on an uplifting note" as propaganda plays are apt to do. There *is* a firmly positive cadence, but it comes a moment earlier, in the two boys' farewells to each other. Here the relationship of Melchior and Moritz—the first relationship defined in the play (I.2)—reveals itself as finest relationship in the play. It is not the passionately gay yet dubiously stable relationship of Hänschen and Ernst. It is durable love without the physically sexual element:

MORITZ: Don't hold it against me that I tried to kill you, Melchior, put it down to lingering affection: I'd gladly moan and groan for the rest of my life if I could go out with you one more time.

MELCHIOR: …How many untroubled happy days we've had in the fourteen years!…Come what may, I shall never forget you!

MORITZ: Thanks, thanks, dear heart!

MELCHIOR: Though I live to be an old man…you may still be closer to me than all the living.

MORITZ: Thank you.

This being the love of two boys, one should not be surprised to hear that the play has irked some feminist critics of the late 20th century. Frank Wedekind is indeed not of *their* era, one more reason why his play should always be presented in period — 1891, not 1991. The protagonist is a male, chiefly shown among other males. The girl he gets pregnant is seen less as part of her life than as part of his. Even when she is shown among other females, what is dramatized is chiefly her (and their) relation to males. All Wedekind wishes for Wendla is maternity, whereas what he wishes for Melchior is more than literal paternity, it is a patriarchal role in mastery of the world. Ideally, Melchior would be a young Goethe, whereas Wendla would have to be satisfied with the role of a humdrum Frau Goethe.

Should Moritz, like the Man in the Mask, be taken as, in the last analysis, part of Melchior? In the first analysis, no, because Moritz represents the Aarau boys who did commit suicide, as against Wedekind-Melchior who did not. The suicide scene (Act 2, Scene 7) parallels the final scene of the play. The dialogue itself spells out the idea that the Man — in his role of Life as the foe of Death — was as much present on the earlier occasion as on the later:

> **MORITZ:** You might have happened on me too . . . as I trudged
> through the alder plantations with a pistol in my pocket.
> **MAN:** You don't remember? Even at the last minute you were
> hesitating between Death and . . . Life.

But more present to Moritz than the silent Man in this scene is
the voluble and temptingly visible Ilse—not Thanatos, she, but
Eros:

> A child of fourteen, I had never
> Had anything to do with boys
> But that's when I made a discovery:
> Sweet as sugar are life's joys.
>
> He laughed and took hold of my body
> This is not gonna hurt, he said
> And then he gently, gently pushed my
> Underskirt above my head.
>
> Since then my life has all been springtime
> And I make love with one and all
> And if the time comes no man wants me
> I'm ready for my funeral.

Thus we see Moritz, here, primarily, as another and different person—different motives, different result. The parallels
between the two scenes are less striking than the contrasts, especially this contrast: Melchior is first offered death but then
chooses life, Moritz is first offered life (Eros) but has irrevocably
chosen death. Moritz, it seems, has a *destiny* which cannot be
gainsaid. Melchior defies fate, and makes his own way in the
world. Which is all in the first analysis. In the last analysis,
Moritz *is* part of Melchior, a part which is later discarded. He
was a part of Wedekind which was not discarded. Early and late,
Wedekind felt himself divided between these two masculine
models which he dubbed "Wedekind and Hauptmann" and
which he presented on an illustrative chart as follows:

Wedekind and Hauptmann

In sketches for a never-finished play called *Niggerjew*, Wedekind characterized himself and Gerhart Hauptmann in the following two columns. (He said the pairing could also be that of Ibsen and Björnson.)

Wedekind/Ibsen	Hauptmann/Björnson
Egoist	Altruist
Night person	Day person
Thinker	Artist
City person	Country person
Culture snob	Child of nature
Calculator	Builder
Lefthanded	Creator
Peer Gynt	Brand
Franz Moor	Karl Moor
Mephisto	Faust
Marquis of Keith	Scholz
Pessimist	Optimist
Lichtalb[2]	Wandering Aryan
Theoretician	Sculptor
Practical, has to fight every step of the way	Ethical, makes a brilliant career as Grand Seigneur
Self-aware	Selfless, preaches the great love [*die grosse Liebe*], pity, tolerance
Authentic but horrible	Enchanting, but inauthentic, inauthenticity mars all he does, joy in the beauty of empty words

2 Literally: Elf of the Light, a term used by the Nibelung, Alberich, in *The Ring*.

ANOTHER KIND OF DRAMA

Spring's Awakening is autobiographical, yet it is not an auto-biography, it is a drama: not monologue, but duologue, not lyric outpouring in a single voice, but conflict actualized by at least two conflicting voices. And this being Wedekindian drama, there is more than one conflict, and we are afforded more than two perspectives on the more than one conflicts along the way.

What *kind* of drama is this? Initially, its fans made the same assumption as its censors: the play is a dramatic pamphlet in behalf of sexual enlightenment. What we now call the Establishment must be against it—since it threatens their existence—and what is now loosely called the Left must be for it, since it represents their very own views. To the Right, this was pornography and anarchy. To the Left, it was truth and freedom. In short, it was initially regarded as political theatre and so radical that it could not be performed in any country that the published script had reached. It reached America, for example, almost at once, and we find a Detroit, Michigan, periodical running a serial review of it—in five weekly installments—as early as 1892, while the first American performance in English would not take place till 1917, and the play would not really be "on the market" till decades later than that.

If the decisions of the various censorships were sweeping and extreme, so were the verdicts of the revolutionary fans such as the great anarchist Emma Goldman whose New York lectures of 1914 contained such language as the following:

> *Spring's Awakening* is one of the great forces of modern times that is paving the way for the birth of a free race.

> *Spring's Awakening* has done much to dispel the mist enveloping the paramount issue of sex in the education of the child.

> . . . Every word in *Spring's Awakening* is vividly true.

> More boldly than any other dramatist Frank Wedekind has laid
> bare the shams of morality in reference to sex, especially attacking
> the ignorance surrounding the sex life of the child and its result-
> ant tragedies.

But even before Emma Goldman spoke these words in New York,
Wedekind himself had complained of the narrowly political-
sociological interpretations of his play, chiefly, of course, those of
the Right:

> Since about 1901, above all since Max Reinhardt put it on stage
> [1906], it has been regarded as an angry, deadly earnest tragedy, as
> a thesis play, as a polemic in the service of sexual enlightenment
> — or whatever the current slogans of the fussy, pedantic lower
> middle class may be.

And, instead, he invites the public to see his play as a humorous
work:

> ...a sunny image of life, in every scene of which [except one] I
> tried to exploit an unburdened humor for all it was worth.

Which is all very well as a corrective, written in 1911, to the view
he is attacking, but is quite inadequate as an account to his own
dramaturgy. In 1891, he had subtitled his play a TRAGEDY of
childhood. In 1911 he asks us to take it as a COMEDY. Thus,
putting two and two together, we can correctly conclude that what
we have here is a tragi-comedy. But a label is not an analysis. Let
us look further.

A Wedekind play, such as this, may be in nineteen scenes but is
not episodic, if that term implies a lack of structure and indiffer-
ence to unity. Cross-references between scenes, persistency of
themes throughout are among the factors that bind together and
unify. The over-arching theme of *Spring's Awakening* is the collision
of Eros and Thanatos. The awakening of spring, alone, would not
give us a drama but only a lyric outburst. What happens here, and
turns a lyric into a tragi-comedy, is that when

spring awakes it does not blossom into summer and quietly fade into autumn. A natural/unnatural catastrophe occurs. Winter arrives, two seasons early, and nips spring in the bud. Two budding adolescents, Wendla and Moritz, are killed.

Wedekind complains that his early audiences did not find the comedy in his writing, but, in being receptive only to the social-revolutionary element, they equally missed the tragedy. Did everything promise to come up roses before the crises arrived which carried off Wendla and Moritz? On the contrary, both characters, from the outset, carry with them a sense of doom. If the comedy in the play stems from Wedekind's lively and affirmative sense of Eros, the tragedy derives from an equally powerful sense of the ubiquity and inevitability of (premature) death. Wendla is characterized from the beginning (I.1) as death-haunted:

> MRS. BERGMANN: Who knows where you'll be when the other girls are fully developed?
> WENDLA: Who knows? Maybe I won't be around.
> MRS. BERGMANN: Child, child, where do you get such ideas?
> WENDLA: They just come to me in the evening when I can't get to sleep.

Then there is Moritz. The plot of *Spring's Awakening* would seem, if such an impossibility can be permitted, to have two centers: the pregnancy and death of Wendla *and* the suicide of Moritz. Reading the account (above) of the actual suicide of Wedekind's schoolfellows, one might expect Moritz's suicide to be the single center of the play. But then one would be expecting a single, linear thread of narrative. The singleness in the play is not in the narrative but in the theme—and in the fact that there is a single center, character-wise, namely Melchior.

The articulation is as follows. All elements in the story lead toward death. We seem headed for a drama which, after such a model as *Danton's Death*—and Wedekind was, with Hauptmann, the first playwright to be markedly influenced by Büchner—will be a Melchior's Death. This continues to be the case right through the action up to the final scene and through that very scene up to the entrance of the Man in the Mask. The Man is the agency through which Melchior turns from death to life. Which leaves Moritz isolated, now, as the sole deathly element.

This result had been carefully prepared by the playwright, as we can confirm by checking back with the first scenes in which Moritz appears. From the outset, life had been too much for him. If we take the play as simply social-revolutionary, Moritz's orientation is to be attributed to pressure from the school authorities. But none of the other boys respond as negatively as Moritz, though they all experience the pressures. His opposite pole is Hänschen Rilow who responds with defiance, and lets himself fully *enjoy* the awakening of spring (even though he teaches himself a degree of restraint in abstaining, on occasion, from masturbation). Moritz is in love with death, though not serenely so. In the final, fantasy scene, Wedekind shows him headless—because he has always been headless, really, had taken one look at the spring, and "lost his head."

The play is full of allusions to Goethe, and, when we first meet Melchior and Moritz we find them trying to read *Faust*. They have only got up to the Walpurgis Night in Part One, and that is where Moritz remains, while Melchior finally becomes, shall we say, one of Goethe's Blessed Boys (*Faust, Part Two*, Act 5) aspiring to perfection. The image of a headless queen is lifted from the passage in the Walpurgis Night where Mephisto says that, now Perseus has cut Medusa's head off, "Sie kann das Haupt auch unterm Arme tragen," "she can even carry her head under her arm."

AND ANOTHER KIND OF
SUBTEXT

It has been said of Shakespeare that he addressed two publics at the same time, giving the groundlings a big show and a grand entertainment while introducing much that is exquisite and profound for connoisseurs only—and for the scholars and critics who make this point. I cannot say exactly the same of Wedekind, yet there is a duality in his work not altogether different. Beneath the main action and dialogue carrying it lies a subtext of literary allusions. I cited the phenomenon in my earlier Notes on *The First Lulu*. In that play, allusions, especially to Wagner and Nietzsche, provide a strange but somehow firm underpinning to the Wedekindian text.

The allusion of allusions in *Spring's Awakening* is to Goethe, and most often to his *Faust*. The later play had two principal points of departure: the schoolboy suicides already cited and the Gretchen tragedy in *Faust*, which Wedekind, feeling perhaps what the critic Harold Bloom calls the anxiety of influence reworks and modernizes: the virginal victim is killed, this time, by abortion pills, the grown-up philanderer Faust is replaced by a child just discovering desire and its sado-masochistic component. But then, as mentioned, *Faust* is the book the two boys are reading in Act II, Scene 1, and a least Moritz would seem to have got stuck at the Walpurgis Night scene. How would he not? Walpurgis Night is April 30, the eve of May Day, an apt date for anyone's springtime awakening. Moritz probably knew that Walpurgis was a woman and a Christian saint, and that no one can figure how her name got mixed up with a Witches Sabbath, but it did, and Moritz would feel: well, that's life . . .

Although Frank Wedekind elsewhere shows himself much devoted to Goethe's idea of an Ewig-Weibliche (Eternal Feminine) which leads us onward and upward, and although his play will

indeed close with a (modified) Onward and Upward sentiment, it
is to another Goethe work that he turns for his Finale, an essay
called "Shakespeare und kein Ende" — Shakespeare without end.
(Herewith anxiety for the most overpowering of literary influences:
that of Shakespeare.) The topic is morality. Both Melchior and
Moritz have been intimidated by the (fake) morality prescribed by
teachers and parents. Moritz destroys himself on that account.
Melchior is reduced to suicidal despair but is then rescued from it
by a Goethean gospel: human beings must disregard the current
models and mores and weigh freedom against necessity, personal
wishes against inexorable fate…

If Goethe's name ranks highest in German poetry, Luther's
Bible ranks highest in German prose, and the second running allusion in *Spring's Awakening*, the second subtext, is biblical: it gives
Wedekind very wide latitude because the Enemy, in his story, are
bibliolaters, while his hero is an anti-hero and therefore an anti-
bibliolator, a "Philistine," a pagan. So biblical language is most
conspicuous in the scene of Moritz's funeral, though it is manipu-
lated there to express ideas foreign both to Judaism and
Christianity, akin however to the ideas of the supposedly Christian
priest in the last act of *Hamlet*:

> PRIEST: She [Ophelia] should in ground unsanctified have lodged
> Till the last trumpet…
> Shards, flints, and pebbles should be thrown on her.

In the Wedekind nightmare, these formulations rise to the pitch of
theological hysteria:

> PASTOR SKINNYTUM: He who has lived and worked for evil in the
> selfwilled carnal denial of the honor which is God's due shall die
> the death of the body, but he who lightly casts from him the
> cross which the All-Merciful has laid upon him for his sins, ver-
> ily, verily I say unto you, he shall die an eternal death!

When Wedekind actually quotes the New Testament, and accurately, he then attributes the "quote" to the wrong chapter and verse:

> PASTOR SKINNYTUM:…all things work together for good to them that love God. I Corinthians 12.15.

No theatre audience is going to pick this up, but that is not what I Corinthians 12.15 says. (It is a correct "quote," but from Romans 8.28.) The Devil can quote Scripture to his purpose, and Wedekind-Mephistopheles is referring us to a passage in I Corinthians 12 where the Apostle is meditating on the status of different parts of the body. (One must have in mind the boys' discovery in Act II, Scene 1 of *Spring's Awakening* that everything revolved around penis and vagina.) All parts of the body are to be held in honor, the Apostle is saying, including those parts which some belittle: "…to those parts of the body which seem to us to be less deserving of notice, we have to allow the highest honor of function. The parts which do not look beautiful have a deeper beauty in the work they do…"

In the theatre, all this must pass the audience by, except for the occasional Bible student who spots a mis-attribution. For the initiated, there is a subtext that ironizes the main text, and leads out of the "melodrama" of the scene into an illumination, an epiphany.

The scene in which sex is most grossly physical is Act III, Scene 4, the Reformatory scene, where the whole bunch of boys masturbate together to see whose sperm will hit a coin on the floor. It is a scene of maximum subtext. By contrast with these animals, Melchior himself, seducer if not rapist of Wendla, is a chaste Joseph, invulnerable to the blandishments of Potiphar's wife. However, he knows that the other lads in jail are sex-mad, so he exploits the sexiest bits of the Old Testament that he can find to keep his friend, Ruprecht, happy. (Details on page 67). Incest seems to be the main theme – not uninteresting if one knows what Melchior's own problems have been.

This biblical, anti-biblical scene ends with a broader and cli-
mactic allusion to Frank Wedekind's favorite book: *Casanova's
Memoirs*. For Casanova readers, no passage is more celebrated
than the account of Casanova's escape from the dungeons of
Venice: it fills several dozen pages. Wedekind provides a mini-
version for his mini-hero, a serious parody, lovingly done, in
which Melchior emerges as a budding Casanova![3]

---

3 The *Memoirs* are not *my* favorite book, and I had to have this allusion point-
ed out to me in the notes of Erhard Weidl.

THE QUESTION OF STYLE

When productions of my version of *Spring's Awakening* come up, I am always asked—usually by the director—about the style, which is to say the mode. To what extent is the play naturalistic, in any definition of that term? And should we call certain scenes expressionistic? If so, is the play in two modes and therefore to be played in two styles?

There is no simple answer. The terms themselves are none too clear, and certainly there is no agreed way of using the words naturalistic and expressionistic. Attempting simplicity neverthe-less, let me invite the prospective director to see the play as beginning in one mode and toward the end moving into anoth-er. Certainly the first is the more natural, literal, everyday mode, and the second is a distortion thereof, yielding, on the one hand, lyricism, as in the vineyard scene and, on the other, the gro-tesque as in the schoolroom and funeral scenes. In the last scene of all, the two modes are united: that is another sense in which this scene is a culmination, bringing together the comedy and the tragedy, the naturalistic, if you will, and the expressionistic.

If there is a style problem in a given production, it will be acute in the final scene, which can either prove, in performance, too heavy or too light, too grim or too pleasant, too actual or too fantastic. Wedekind has spoken of his play as full of sunshine from beginning to end, yet Wedekind, acting the Man in the Mask, was criticized for making the role too forbidding and hor-rible. He, of course, saw something diabolonian (Shaw's word) in the character, and in any event, as on the chart above, saw himself not as a Faust but as a Mephisto. It is a question of bal-ance. The Man in the Mask is a counter-figure to that false morality which has brought Wendla, Moritz, and Melchior to their present pass. By that token he is a counter-figure to parent, teacher, and priest as we have seen them. His version of the Devil must match, and try to outmatch, their version of God. Can one translate such an understanding of his character into purely stylistic terms? Not with any precision; and yet—in his instructions to others, whether actors, designers, costumers—the stage director needs to be precise. It is just that a style is not arrived at through the understanding, either the playwright's or the director's or the actor's. At this point, such commentary as this of mine loses its usefulness (assuming it has one). The precisions, the rightnesses—the style—of a production of *Spring's Awakening* will emerge, if at all, as a by-product of the rehearsal process, a by-product of concentrated work on the dramatic elements which I have here set forth.

SPRING'S AWAKENING

Tragedy of Childhood

CHARACTERS

MRS. BERGMANN
    WENDLA BERGMAN }   her daughters
    INA MÜLLER

MR.GABOR
MRS. GABOR
   MELCHIOR   their son

RENTIER[1] STIEFEL
   MORITZ STIEFEL   his son

OTTO
GEORG
ROBERT }   schoolboys
ERNST
LÄMMERMEIER
HÄNSCHEN RILOW[2]

THEA }
MARTHA }   schoolgirls

ILSE   a model

REKTOR SONNENSTICH (Sunstroke)
AFENSCHMALZ (Calflove)
KNÜPPELDICK (Thickstick)
HUNGERGURT (Starveling) }   schoolmasters
ZUNGENSCHLAG (Stickytongue)
KNOCHENBRUCH (Bonebreaker)
FLIEGENTOD (Flykiller)

HABEBALD (Catchmequick)   school porter

---

1 German title for one who lives on a private income (rents and dividends).
2 If actors cannot pronounce "Hänschen", he could be called Hansi (little Hans).

PASTOR KAHLBAUCH (Skinnytum)
FRIEND ZIEGENMELKER (Goatmilker)
UNCLE PROBST (Provost)

DIETHELM
REINHOLD
RUPRECHT } boys in the reformatory
HELMUTH
GASTON

DR. PROCRUSTES
LOCKSMITH
DR. VON BRAUSEPULVER (Fizzpowder)
VINTAGERS
A MAN IN A MASK

THE TIME: 1892
THE PLACE: GERMANY

A Note on the Language: It is a pity the term "period piece" carries overtones that are wholly unfavorable. For a piece like this is still full of life, while belonging unmistakably to an earlier period. While I have not attempted to reproduce the speech of 1891 with exactitude, neither have I tried to give the effect of a late twentieth century. Even as of 1891, Wedekind's language is peculiar. His background was international, and his German has no single regional root. By consequence, it is always a little abstract and more than a little idiosyncratic. In addition, his children's talk is the talk, very often, of children pretending to be grown up. The awkwardness of adolescent gestures is a familiar enough fact: Wedekind explored the awkwardness of adolescent speech. Adolescents of Germany, 1891, differ from the adolescents of America, 1995, in carrying a much heavier load of Culture. Some of Wedekind's children know more literature than of life.

ACT I

SCENE 1

A living room. WENDLA BERGMANN *and her mother.*

WENDLA: Why have you made my dress so long, Mother?

MRS. BERGMANN: You're fourteen today.

WENDLA: If I'd known you were going to make my dress as long as that I'd rather have stayed thirteen.

MRS. BERGMANN: The dress isn't too long, Wendla. What do you expect? I can't help it if my daughter is an inch taller every spring. A big girl like you can't go around in a little-girl dress.

WENDLA: The little-girl dress suits me better than that old sack. — Let me wear it a little longer, Mother! Just for the summer! This penitential robe will keep. —Hold it till my next birthday. I'd only trip on the hem now.

MRS. BERGMANN: I don't know what to say. I'd like to keep you exactly as you are, child. Other girls are gawky and gangling at your age. You're just the opposite. —Who knows what you'll be like when the others are fully developed?

WENDLA: Who knows? Maybe I won't be around.

MRS. BERGMANN: Child, child, where do you get such ideas?

WENDLA: Oh, Mother, please don't be sad!

MRS. BERGMANN: [*Kissing her.*] My little precious!

WENDLA: Such ideas come to me in the evening when I can't go to sleep. And I don't feel sad, either. I know I'll sleep all the better. –Is it sinful to think such things, Mother?

MRS. BERGMANN: Oh, all right, go and hang the penitential robe in the closet and put your little-girl dress on again if you must. —When I have time I'll put a strip of flouncing on it.

WENDLA: [*Hanging the dress in the cupboard.*] Oh, no! In that case, I'd rather be twenty right away!

MRS. BERGMANN: I only hope you won't be cold. —That little dress *was* long enough, but...

WENDLA: What, now, with summer coming on? —Oh, Mother, a girl doesn't get diphtheria in the back of her knees, why so fainthearted? You don't feel the cold at my age, specially not in the legs. And would it be any better if I was too hot, Mother? —You can think yourself lucky if one fine morning your little precious doesn't cut her sleeves off or come home in the evening without shoes and stockings. —When I wear my penitential robe I'll be dressed like the queen of the fairies underneath...Don't scold, Mother darling. No one will ever see it!

SCENE 2

Out of doors. Sunday evening. MELCHIOR, MORITZ, OTTO, GEORG, ROBERT, ERNST.

MELCHIOR: This is boring. I'm going to stop playing.

OTTO: Then the rest of us will have to stop too! —Have you done the homework, Melchior?

MELCHIOR: *You* don't have to stop.

MORITZ: Where are you going?

MELCHIOR: For a walk.

GEORG: But it's getting dark!

ROBERT: Finished your homework already?

MELCHIOR: Why shouldn't I take a walk in the dark?

ERNST: Central America! Louis the Fifteenth! —Sixty lines of Homer! —Seven equations!

MELCHIOR: This damned homework!

GEORG: If only that Latin exercise wasn't for tomorrow!

MORITZ: One can't think of anything without homework getting in the way.

OTTO: I'm going home.

GEORG: Me too. Homework!

ERNST: Me too.

ROBERT: G'night, Melchior.

MELCHIOR: G'night.

[*All leave but* MORITZ. *and* MELCHIOR.]

MELCHIOR: [*Cont'd.*] What I'd like to know is: why do we exist?

MORITZ: I'd rather be a cab horse than have to go to school! —Why *do* we go? —We go to school to take exams! —And why do they examine us? —So they can flunk us! —They have to flunk seven—the classroom above only holds sixty. —I've felt so strange since Christmas . . . If it wasn't for Father, damned if I wouldn't pack my bag and head for Hamburg!

MELCHIOR: Let's talk about something else.

[*They take a walk.*]

MORITZ: Did you see that black cat with its tail in the air?

MELCHIOR: You believe in omens?

MORITZ: I'm not sure. —She came over from the other side. Doesn't mean a thing, of course.

MELCHIOR: Pull free of the Scylla of religious delusion, and you fall victim to the Charybdis of superstition! —Let's sit under this beech tree. A warm breeze is blowing in from the mountains. How I wish I were a young dryad up there in the forest tossed and cradled all night long in the topmost branches!

MORITZ: Unbutton your vest, Melchior.

MELCHIOR: Ah! How it blows one's clothes around!

MORITZ: Darned if it isn't getting so dark you can't see your hand before your face. Where are you actually? —Don't you agree, Melchior, that the sense of shame is simply a product of a person's upbringing?

MELCHIOR: I was thinking about that the day before yesterday. But I must say it seems to me rooted in human nature. Imagine having to undress—completely—in front of your best friend. You wouldn't, unless he did. —Then again, it's more or less a question of fashion.

MORITZ: If I have children, I'll have them sleep in the same room from the start. If possible in the same bed. Boys *and* girls. I'll make them help each other dress and undress, and in hot weather boys as well as girls will wear nothing but a short white, woolen tunic with a leather belt. —Brought up like this, they'll be, well, less disturbed that we usually are.

MELCHIOR: I'm sure you're right, Moritz. —The only question is, when the girls have babies, what then?

MORITZ: How do you mean, have babies?

MELCHIOR: Well, if you ask me, I believe there's some kind of instinct at work. For example, if you took two kittens, a he and a she, and shut them up together for life, and never let any other cats in—in short you left them entirely to their instincts—I believe that, sooner or later, the she-cat would become pregnant—even though neither she nor the tom has had any opportunity to learn by example.

MORITZ: I suppose you're right. With animals it must come all by itself.

MELCHIOR: With humans too! That's *my* theory. May I ask, Moritz, when your boys sleep in the same bed as the girls, and then suddenly feel... the first stirrings of their manhood, well, I bet anything—

MORITZ: You may be right. —Even so...

MELCHIOR: And at the corresponding age exactly the same thing would happen to your girls! Not that girls are exactly... it's hard to judge precisely... anyway we can certainly assume... and curiosity can be relied on to play its part!

MORITZ: By the way, I have a question.

MELCHIOR: Well?

MORITZ: Will you answer it?

MELCHIOR: Of course!

MORITZ: Really?

MELCHIOR: Cross my heart! —Well, Moritz?

MORITZ: Have you done the exercise yet?

MELCHIOR: Oh, come on! There's no one to see or hear us!

MORITZ: Naturally, my children will have to work all day either in the garden or at the farm or amuse themselves with games that provide physical exercise. Riding, climbing, gymnastics... Above all they mustn't sleep on such soft beds as we do. Those beds have made us soft. —I don't believe you dream if you sleep on a hard bed.

MELCHIOR: From now till after grape harvest I'll be sleeping exclusively in my hammock. I've put my bed behind the stove. It folds up. —Once last winter I dreamt I'd been flogging our dog Lolo so long he couldn't move his legs. That's the most horrible thing I ever dreamt. —Why are you looking at me like that?

MORITZ: Have you felt them yet?

MELCHIOR: What?

MORITZ: What did you call them?

MELCHIOR: The stirrings of manhood?

MORITZ: Uh, huh.

MELCHIOR: —Certainly!

MORITZ: Me too. - ³

MELCHIOR: I've know for ages. —A year at least!

MORITZ: I felt like I'd been struck by lightning.

MELCHIOR: You'd had a dream?

MORITZ: A short one ... About legs in sky-blue tights climbing over the lectern. At least I *think* that's what they were trying to do. —I only caught a glimpse of them.

MELCHIOR: George Zirschnitz dreamt of his mother.

MORITZ: Did he tell you so?

MELCHIOR: Out on Gallows Lane.

MORITZ: If you only knew what I've been through since that night!

MELCHIOR: The prickings of conscience?

---

3 Here and in what follows, the translator has retained the dashes Wedekind inserts at points where feeling goes beyond verbal expression. What actors make of these signals is up to them.

MORITZ: Prickings of conscience? - - - - - - - The fear of death!

MELCHIOR: Good God!

MORITZ: I thought there was no hope for me. I was sure I must be suffering from some internal complaint. —In the end I calmed down, but only because I began to write my memoirs. Yes, my dear Melchior, the last three weeks have been my Gethsemane.

MELCHIOR: When it happened to me I was more or less prepared for it. I was a bit ashamed. —But that was all.

MORITZ: And yet you're almost a year younger than me!

MELCHIOR: I wouldn't worry about that, Moritz, in my experience, there's no fixed time for the arrival of these... phantoms. You know the big Lämmermeier boy with the straw-colored hair and the hooked nose? He's three years older than me. Hänschen Rilow says that he still dreams of nothing but pound cake and apricot jelly.

MORITZ: Now how can Hänschen Rilow know that?

MELCHIOR: He asked him.

MORITZ: He asked him? —I'd never dare *ask* anyone!

MELCHIOR: You asked *me*.

MORITZ: So I did—It wouldn't surprise me if Hänschen had even made his will! —A strange game they play with us. And we're supposed to be grateful. I can't recall ever feeling any longing for excitements of this kind. Why didn't they let me sleep quietly on till everything had calmed down again? My dear parents could have had a hundred better children than me. Yet here I am, I don't know how I got here, and I'm supposed to answer for not having stayed away. —Haven't you ever wondered, Melchior, how we got into this whirlpool actually?

11

MELCHIOR: You still don't know, Moritz?

MORITZ: How should I know? —I see that hens lay eggs, and I hear that Mama carried me under her heart. Is that enough? And I can remember, even as a child of five, feeling embarrassed if anyone turned up the queen of hearts: she wore décolleté. That feeling has gone. On the other hand, today I can scarcely talk to any girl without thinking something disgusting—though, I swear to you, Melchior, I don't know what.

MELCHIOR: I'll tell you everything. —I got it partly from books, partly from pictures, partly from observing nature. You'll be surprised: it made an atheist of me for a time. —I told George Zirschnitz. Georg wanted to tell Hänschen Rilow but Hänschen learnt it all from his governess when he was a kid.

MORITZ: I've been through Meyer's *Lexicon* from A to Z. Words! Nothing but words! Not one simple explanation. Oh this sense of shame! —What's the good of an encyclopedia that doesn't answer the most pertinent question in the world?

MELCHIOR: Have you, for instance, ever seen two dogs running together across the street?

MORITZ: No! - - - - Don't tell me any more today, Melchior. I still have Central America and Louis the Fifteenth to take care of. And on top of that the sixty verses of Homer, the seven equations, the Latin exercise. I'd only flunk everything again tomorrow. To get anywhere with my studies, I'll have to develop a thick hide.

MELCHIOR: Come back to my room. In three-quarters of an hour I'll whip through the Homer, the equations, and *two* exercises. I'll slip in a few harmless mistakes for you, and this job's done. Mama will make us some of her lemonade, and we'll have a nice relaxed talk about reproduction.

MORITZ: I can't. —I can't relax on a subject like reproduction. If you want to do me a favor, give me your explanations in writing. Write down what you know. Make it as brief and clear as you can and stick it among my books during gym. I'll take it home without knowing I've got it. I'll come upon it unexpectedly. I'll have no choice but to glance through it . . . with a weary eye . . . and if it's absolutely necessary, you could add a few illustrations in the margin.

MELCHIOR: You're like a girl. —But just as you say. It's quite an interesting assignment. —One question, Moritz.

MORITZ: Hm?

MELCHIOR: —Have you ever *seen* a girl?

MORITZ: Yes, I have!

MELCHIOR: All of her?

[MORITZ *nods*.]

MELCHIOR: [*Cont'd.*] Me too. —Then illustrations won't be needed.

MORITZ: During the Shooting Contest. In Leilich's Anatomical Museum. If they'd ever found out, they'd have thrown me out of school. —Beautiful as sunlight! And quite natural!

MELCHIOR: Last summer I was with mother in Frankfort and— Do you have to be going, Moritz?

MORITZ: Homework! —G'night.

MELCHIOR: So long.

SCENE 3

THEA, WENDLA, *and* MARTHA *come up the street arm in arm.*

MARTHA: How the water gets into your shoes!

WENDLA: How the wind whistles about your cheeks!

THEA: How your heart beats!

WENDLA: Let's go out to the bridge. Ilse says the river's sweeping plants and trees along. The boys have a raft on the water. They say Melchi Gabor nearly got drowned last night.

THEA: Oh, he can swim.

MARTHA: I should say so!

WENDLA: If he hadn't been able to, he'd have drowned.

THEA: Your braid's coming undone, Martha, your braid's coming undone!

MARTHA: Pooh, let it! It's a nuisance—all day and all night. I'm not allowed to wear my hair short like yours or loose like Wendla's. I can't wear bangs. I have to braid it even at home. All because of my parents.

WENDLA: I'll bring a pair of scissors to Bible class tomorrow. And while we're reciting "Blessed is the man that walketh"[4] I'll cut it.

MARTHA: For heaven's sake, Wendla! Papa would beat me black and blue, and Mama would lock me in the coalhole three nights on end.

WENDLA: What does he beat you with, Martha?

MARTHA: I sometimes think they'd feel something was missing if they didn't have a little mess like me for a daughter.

THEA: But Martha!

MARTHA: Some of you were allowed to thread a blue ribbon through the yoke of your nightdress, weren't you?

4 Opening words of Psalm I in the Bible.

THEA: Mine's pink satin! Mama maintains that pink suits me—with my coal-black eyes.

MARTHA: Blue looked so lovely on me! —Mama pulled me out of bed by my braids. I fell on the floor with my hands out like this. —Mama prays with us every evening...

WENDLA: If I were you I'd have run away long ago.

MARTHA: ... "So that's it, that's what you have in mind!" she says. "Well, I just wanted to see it, I just wanted to see it. At least," says she, "you'll have nothing to reproach your mother with later..."

THEA: Oh, won't you?

MARTHA: Can you imagine what mother meant by that, Thea?

THEA: I can't. — Can you, Wendla?

WENDLA: I'd have asked her.

MARTHA: I lay on the floor and shrieked and yelled. Enter papa. Rip! Off comes my nightdress! I head for the door. "So that's it," he shouts, "you'd like to go out like that, wouldn't you?"

WENDLA: Oh, now you're telling stories, Martha!

MARTHA: It was freezing. I went back in. I had to spend the whole night on the floor in a sack.

THEA: I could never sleep in a sack as long as I live.

WENDLA: I'd be glad to sleep in your sack for you.

MARTHA: It's only the beatings...

THEA: Oh, it's enough to stifle you to death.

MARTHA: Your head sticks out. You tie the sack under your chin.

THEA: And then they beat you?

MARTHA: No. Only when there's something special.

WENDLA: What do they beat you with, Martha?

MARTHA: Oh, I don't know. Anything. — Does *your* mother think it's indecent to eat in bed?

WENDLA: Oh, no!

MARTHA: I suppose they have fun, though they never mentioned it. — If I ever have children I'll let them grow like the weeds in our flower garden. No one bothers about them and they're so thick, so tall, while the roses — staked out in those beds — bloom more miserably every summer.

THEA: If I have children I'll dress them all in pink. Pink hats, pink dresses, pink shoes. Only the stockings — the stockings shall be as black as night. And when I take them out I'll make them all walk in front of me. —What about you, Wendla?

WENDLA: You both know if you're going to have some?

THEA: Why shouldn't we have some?

MARTHA: Well, Aunt Euphemia hasn't got any.

THEA: Because she's not *married*, silly.

WENDLA: My Aunt Bauer's been married three times and hasn't got a single one.

MARTHA: If you have some, Wendla, which would you rather have, boys or girls?

WENDLA: Boys! Boys!

THEA: Boys for me too!

MARTHA: Me too! I'd rather have twenty boys than three girls.

THEA: Girls are boring.

MARTHA: If I hadn't been a girl up to now I certainly wouldn't want to become one.

WENDLA: I think that's a matter of taste, Martha! I give thanks every day that I'm a girl. Believe me, I wouldn't change places with a king's son. — I want to *have* sons!

THEA: That's a lot of nonsense, Wendla, just nonsense!

WENDLA: But surely, Thea, it must be a thousand times more inspiring to be loved by a man than by a girl!

THEA: You don't mean to tell me Forestry Commissioner Pfälle loves Melitta more than she loves him?

WENDLA: I certainly do, Thea. — Pfälle is proud of being Forestry Commissioner, he doesn't have money. Melitta is radiantly happy because she gets ten thousand times more than she gives.

MARTHA: Aren't you proud — of yourself, Wendla?

WENDLA: That would be foolish.

MARTHA: How proud *I'd* be in your shoes.

THEA: Just see how she places her feet, how she looks straight ahead, how she carries herself Martha! — If that isn't pride!

WENDLA: But what for? I'm so happy to be a girl. If I weren't a girl I'd kill myself –so that the next time…

[MELCHIOR *passes and greets them.*]

THEA: He has a marvelous head.

MARTHA: That's how I picture the young Alexander when he was a pupil of Aristotle's.

THEA: Oh Lord, Greek history! All I can remember is how Socrates lay in the barrel when Alexander sold him the ass' shadow.[5]

5 Thea has confused Socrates with Diogenes and has mixed in the quite other fable of the sale of an ass' shadow. Latent in this mix-up is an image of Melchior as man of action or realist (Alexander, Aristotle) and Moritz as idealist (Socrates, Diogenes).

WENDLA: He's supposed to be third in his class.

THEA: Professor Bonebreaker says if he wanted to he could be first.

MARTHA: He has a lovely forehead, but his friend has a more spiritual look.

THEA: Moritz Stiefel? —*He'll* never be anybody!

MARTHA: I get on with him quite well.

THEA: He always does something embarrassing. At the children's party the Rilows gave he offered me some chocolates. Just imagine, Wendla, they were soft and warm! Isn't that . . . ? — He said he'd had them too long in his trouser pocket!

WENDLA: Just think, Melchi Gabor told me that night he didn't believe in anything: God, an afterlife, or anything at all.

SCENE 4

A park in front of school. —MELCHIOR, OTTO, GEORG, ROBERT, HÄNSCHEN RILOW, LÄMMERMEIER.

MELCHIOR: Can any of you tell me where Moritz Stiefel's hiding?

GEORG: He's headed for trouble. Oh, he's headed for trouble!

OTTO: He goes on and on till he's in the soup!

LÄMMERMEIER: A little bird tells me I wouldn't care to be in that man's shoes!

ROBERT: What a nerve! —What absolute gall!

MELCHIOR: Wha . . . wha . . . what is it you all know?

GEORG: What do we know? —Well, let's see—

LÄMMERMEIER: I'm not talking.

OTTO: Nor me. Good God!

MELCHIOR: If you don't tell me right now...

ROBERT: In short: Moritz Stiefel got into the Faculty Room.

MELCHIOR: The Faculty Room?

OTTO: The Faculty Room. Right after Latin class.

GEORG: He stayed behind on purpose.

LÄMMERMEIER: As I turned the corner I saw him open the door.

MELCHIOR: The devil take it...!

LÄMMERMEIER: If only the devil doesn't take *him*!

GEORG: The Rektor must've forgotten to take the key away.

ROBERT: Or else Moritz Stiefel has a skeleton key.

OTTO: I wouldn't put it past him.

LÄMMERMEIER: At best, he'll be kept in on Sunday afternoon.

ROBERT: Also a remark on his report card!

OTTO: Provided he isn't kicked out—with the report *he'll* get.

HÄNSCHEN RILOW: There he is.

MELCHIOR: White as a sheet.

[*Enter* MORITZ, *greatly agitated.*]

LÄMMERMEIER: Moritz, Moritz, what you have done!

MORITZ: —Nothing—Nothing—

ROBERT: You're feverish!

MORITZ: —With happiness—bliss—jubilation.

OTTO: Did they catch you?

MORITZ: I've got my promotion! Melchior, I've got my promotion! —Now the world can come to an end! —I've got my promotion! —Who would have thought I'd get my promotion!—I can't take it in even now! —I've read it twenty times. —I can't believe it—great God, it was still there, it was still there! I've got my promotion! [*Smiling.*] I don't know—I feel so strange—the ground's going up and down...Melchior, Melchior, if you knew what I've been through!

HÄNSCHEN RILOW: Congratulations, Moritz. —Be glad you got away with it.

MORITZ: You've no idea how much was at stake, Hänschen, how could you? For the past three weeks I've been slinking past that door as if it was the jaws of Hell. And today, there it was, unlocked. I think if someone had offered me a million—no, nothing could have stopped me! —So there I am in the middle of the room, I open the register, turn the pages, find the place—and the whole time...it makes me shudder—

MELCHIOR: ...The whole time what?

MORITZ: The whole time the door was standing wide open behind me. How I got out...how I got down the stairs I don't know.

HÄNSCHEN RILOW: —Has Ernst Röbel got his promotion too?

MORITZ: Oh, surely, Hänschen, surely! Ernst Röbel is up too!

ROBERT: That just shows you must have read the thing wrong. Not counting the dunce's bench, with you and Röbel we come to sixty-one, and the classroom upstairs won't hold more than sixty.

MORITZ: I read it right! Ernst Röbel is going up just like me. But it's only provisional. The first term decides which of us must give up his place to the other. —Poor Röbel! —Heaven knows I no longer fear for myself. I've been looking too deep into things for that!

OTTO: I bet you five marks you'll give up the place.

MORITZ: You haven't a penny, and I wouldn't want to rob you. —God, how I'll grind from now on. Now I can tell you all—whether you believe it or not—nothing matters any more—I-I know how true it is: if I didn't get my promotion I was going to shoot myself!

ROBERT: Show-off!

GEORG: Yellow-belly!

OTTO: I'd like to see you shoot *anything!*

LÄMMERMEIER: I bet you a smack in the eye.

MELCHIOR: [*Gives him one.*] —Come on, Moritz. Let's go to the keeper's cottage.

GEORG: You don't believe that stuff?

MELCHIOR: Mind your business. —Let them gab, Moritz. Let's get out! Into town!

[PROFESSORS STARVELING *and* BONEBREAKER *pass by.*]

BONEBREAKER: That my best student should feel himself attracted to my worst is quite incomprehensible to me, dear colleague.

STARVELING: To me also, dear colleague.

SCENE 5

A sunny afternoon. MELCHIOR *and* WENDLA *meet in the woods.*

MELCHIOR: Is it really you, Wendla? —What are you doing all alone up here? —I've been roaming through the woods for the last three hours without meeting a soul and suddenly you pop out of the thickest thicket!

WENDLA: Yes, it's me.

MELCHIOR: If I didn't know you were Wendla Bergmann I'd take you for a dryad from the branches!

WENDLA: No, no, I'm Wendla Bergmann. —What are you doing here?

MELCHIOR: Having my own thoughts.

WENDLA: I'm looking for woodruff. Mama wants to make May wine. At first she wanted to come too, but at the last moment my Aunt Bauer paid us a visit, and she doesn't like to walk uphill. —So I came by myself.

MELCHIOR: Did you find your woodruff?

WENDLA: A basketful. Over there under the bushes it's as thick as clover. —As a matter of fact, I'm looking for a way out, I seem to have got lost. Can you tell me what time it is?

MELCHIOR: Just after half past three. —When are they expecting you?

WENDLA: I thought it was later. I lay a long time in the moss by the stream, just dreaming. The time went so fast. I was afraid evening might be coming on.

MELCHIOR: If they're not expecting you yet, let's lie here a bit longer. Under the oak tree there is my favorite spot. If you lean your head back against the trunk and look up at the sky though the branches you're hypnotized. The ground is still warm from the morning sun. —I've been wanting to ask you something for weeks, Wendla.

WENDLA: I must be home by five.

MELCHIOR: We'll go together. I'll carry the basket, we'll take the path through the gully, and in ten minutes we'll be on the bridge! —When you lie here with your head in your hands you have the strangest thoughts...

[*Both lie down under the oak.*]

WENDLA: What did you want to ask me, Melchior?

MELCHIOR: I heard that you often visit the poor, Wendla. That you take them food and clothes and money. Do you do it of your own accord, or does your mother send you?

WENDLA: Usually mother sends me. They're poor day laborers with a mob of children. Often the man can't find work, and they go cold and hungry. At home we've got all sorts of things in closets and chests, things we don't use, that are just piling up ... But what made you think of it?

MELCHIOR: When your mother sends you somewhere like that do you like to go or not?

WENDLA: I love to go, of course! —How can you ask?

MELCHIOR: The children are dirty, the women are ill, their houses are full of vermin, the men hate you because you don't work ...

WENDLA: That's not true, Melchior. And if it was, all the more reason for me to go.

MELCHIOR: What makes you say that, Wendla?

WENDLA: —It would make me even happier to be able to do something for them.

MELCHIOR: So you visit the poor for your own pleasure?

WENDLA: I visit them because they're poor.

MELCHIOR: But would you go if it didn't give you pleasure?

WENDLA: Can I help it if it gives me pleasure?

MELCHIOR: At that you get yourself into heaven by it. —It's true, then, this thought that's been eating at me for the past month. —Can a man help it if he's closefisted and it *doesn't* give him pleasure to visit dirty, sick children?

WENDLA: It would certainly give you a lot of pleasure!

MELCHIOR: He's supposed to die an eternal death because it doesn't. —I shall write a treatise and send it to Pastor Skinnytum. He's the cause of it all. How he drools about the joys of self-sacrifice! —If he can't answer me I shall stop going to catechism class, I shall refuse to be confirmed.

WENDLA: Why hurt your parents like that? Go through with your confirmation. It won't cost you your head. If it wasn't for our horrid white dresses and your long pants it could even be something to get excited about.

MELCHIOR: There's no such thing as sacrifice! No such thing as unselfishness! —I see the virtuous rejoicing and the wicked trembling and groaning—I see you, Wendla Bergmann, shaking your curls and laughing, and I can't join in because I feel like an outlaw! —What were you dreaming of just now, Wendla, in the grass by the stream?

WENDLA: —Nonsense—foolishness—

MELCHIOR: With your eyes open?

WENDLA: I dreamt I was a poor, poor beggar child. I was sent into the streets at five in the morning. I had to beg all day, in rain and storm, among rough hardhearted people, and if I came home in the evening, shivering with hunger and cold, and didn't bring as much money as my father expected, I'd get beaten—beaten—

MELCHIOR: I know all about that, Wendla. You have those stupid children's stories to thank for it. Believe me, such brutal people don't exist anymore.

WENDLA: They do, Melchior, you're wrong—Martha Bessel gets beaten night after night. Next day you can see the welts. What she must have to suffer! It makes your blood boil to hear her talk about it. I pity her so, I often cry into my pillow in the middle of the night. I've been wondering for months how we could help her. I'd gladly take her place for a week or so.

MELCHIOR: Someone should report her father. They'd take the girl away from him.

WENDLA: I've never been beaten in my life, Melchior. Not once. I can hardly imagine what it's like to be beaten. I've tried beating myself to find out how it feels inside. —It must be a shuddery sensation.

MELCHIOR: I don't believe a child is ever the better for it.

WENDLA: Better for what?

MELCHIOR: For being beaten.

WENDLA: —With this switch for instance? —Phew, it's thin and tough!

MELCHIOR: It would draw blood.

WENDLA: Wouldn't you like to hit me with it once?

MELCHIOR: Hit who?

WENDLA: Hit me.

MELCHIOR: What's got into you, Wendla?

WENDLA: I bet there's nothing to it.

MELCHIOR: Oh, don't worry. I *won't* hit you.

WENDLA: Not if I let you?

MELCHIOR: Never, girl.

WENDLA: Not if I ask you to, Melchior?

MELCHIOR: Are you out of your mind?

WENDLA: I've never been beaten in my life.

MELCHIOR: You can't *ask* for a thing like that...

WENDLA: Please! Please!

MELCHIOR: I'll teach you to say please!

[*He beats her.*]

WENDLA: Oh dear. I don't feel a thing!

MELCHIOR: I believe you. With all those skirts on.

WENDLA: Then hit me on the legs.

MELCHIOR: Wendla!

[*He hits her harder.*]

WENDLA: You're just stroking me! —You're stroking me!

MELCHIOR: Just wait, you little witch, I'll beat the hell out of you!

[*He throws the branch away and pommels her with his fists till she breaks out in fearful yelling. Not in the least deterred, he lets fly at her in a rage, while his tears run down his cheeks. Suddenly he springs upright, clasps his temples with both hands, and plunges into the woods sobbing pitifully and from the depths of his soul.*]

ACT II

SCENE 1

Evening in MELCHIOR'*s study. The window is open. There is a lighted lamp on the table—*MELCHIOR *and* MORITZ *on the sofa.*

MORITZ: Now I'm quite cheerful again, only a little excited. — But in Greek class I slept like the drunken Polyphemus. I'm surprised old Stickytongue didn't pull my ears. —This morning I was within an inch of being late. —My first thought on waking was of the verbs in *mi*. Christ Almighty, Hell and Damnation—all during breakfast and on the way to school I was conjugating till my head swam. —I must have dropped off just after three. On top of everything, my pen had made a blot on the book. The lamp was smoking when Mathilda woke me. The thrushes were twittering in the lilac bushes below, so glad to be alive, and I started feeling indescribably melancholy again. I put my collar on and drew the brush through my hair. —But you feel so good when you've won a victory over yourself.

MELCHIOR: May I roll you a cigarette?

MORITZ: Thank you, I don't smoke. —If only I can go on like this! I mean to work and work till my eyes pop out of my head. —Ernst Röbel has already failed six times since the vacation, three times in Greek, twice with Bonebreaker, and the last time in Lit. I've only been in that unfortunate situation five times, and from now on it's not going to happen again! —Röbel won't shoot himself. Röbel hasn't got parents who are sacrificing their all for him. He can be a mercenary if he wants to, or a sailor or a cowboy. If *I* don't get through, Papa will have a stroke and Mama will go to the madhouse.

27

That's more than a fellow could bear. —Before the exam I asked God to make me consumptive so that the cup might pass from me. It *has* passed. But even now it kind of glimmers at me from a distance, so I don't dare to raise my eyes, day or night. —Having taken hold of the pole I'll hoist myself up all right. My surety for that is the inescapable fact that I can't fall without breaking my neck.

MELCHIOR: Life's meaner than one could ever have expected. I wouldn't mind hanging myself from a branch. —Where can Mama be with the tea!

MORITZ: Your tea will do me good, Melchior. I'm trembling. I feel so strangely disembodied. Just touch me. I see—I hear—I feels so much more clearly—and yet everything's so like a dream—there's such an atmosphere. —The way the park stretches away in the moonlight—so still, so deep, as if into infinity. Dim figures step out, from behind bushes, hurry with breathless haste across the clearings and disappear into the semi-darkness. It seems to me there's a council meeting on under the chestnut tree. —Shall we go down, Melchior?

MELCHIOR: Let's wait till we've had our tea.

MORITZ: —The leaves are whispering so busily. —It's like hearing Grandmother happily telling the story of the queen that had no head. —She was a fabulously beautiful queen, beautiful as the sun, more beautiful than any other girl in the country. Only she'd had the bad luck to be born without a head. She couldn't eat or drink, couldn't see or laugh, she couldn't kiss. She was able to communicate with her attendants only by means of her soft little hand. With her delicate feet she tapped out declarations of war and sentences of death. Then one day she was conquered by a king who happened to have two heads that got in each other's hair all the year round and quarreled so excitedly that neither let the other get a word in edgewise. So the chief court magician took the smaller of the two heads and placed it on the queen. "And lo! It became her passing well." Whereupon the king married the queen, and the two heads no longer got in each other's hair but kissed each other on brow, cheeks, and lips, and lived many years in happiness and joy... What damn nonsense! Since the vacation I can't get the headless queen out of my head. If I see a beautiful girl, I see her without a head, then suddenly I myself seem to be a headless queen... Perhaps I'll get me another head, though.

[*Enter* MRS. GABOR *with the steaming tea, which she places on the table in front of* MORITZ *and* MELCHIOR.]

MRS. GABOR: Here you are, boys, I hope you enjoy it. —Hello, Mr. Stiefel, how are you?

MORITZ: Fine, thanks, Mrs. Gabor. —I was just listening to the goings-on down in the park.

MRS. GABOR: You don't look at all well. —Are you feeling ill?

MORITZ: It doesn't mean a thing. I've been to bed rather late the last few times.

MELCHIOR: Just think: he worked all through the night.

MRS. GABOR: But you shouldn't do such things, Mr. Stiefel. You must look after yourself. School is not a substitute for health. —Plenty of walks in the fresh air! At your age that's more important than accuracy in Middle High German!

MORITZ: I'll take plenty of walks. You're right. And one can work while walking. Why didn't I think of that myself? —Even so, I'd have the written work to do at home.

MELCHIOR: You can do the written work with me: that will make it easier for us both. —Did you know Max von Trenk has died of brain fever, Mama? —This morning Hänschen Rilow came to Rektor Sunstroke from Trenk's deathbed. To report that Max had just died in his presence. —"Really?" said Sunstroke, "don't you still have two hours' detention to do from last week? —Here's the ticket for the school porter. See to it that the matter is finally settled! The whole class will attend the funeral!"—Hänschen was stunned.

MRS. GABOR: What's that book you have there, Melchior?

MELCHIOR: *Faust.*

MRS. GABOR: Have you read it?

MELCHIOR: Not to the end.

MORITZ: We're in the Walpurgis Night.

MRS. GABOR: If I were your age, I'd have waited another year or two.

MELCHIOR: I never found so much in a book before, Mama. It's beautiful. Why shouldn't I read it?

MRS. GABOR: —Because you don't understand it.

MELCHIOR: You can't know that, Mama. I realize I'm in no position to get all the... grandeur of it—

MORITZ: We always read together. Amazing how much more you understand.

MRS. GABOR: You're old enough to know what's good for you, Melchior. Do whatever you can answer to yourself for. I shall be the first to welcome the time when you give me no further reason to hold things back. —I only wanted to point out that even the best can be dangerous when one lacks the maturity to interpret it correctly. —But I'd always rather put my trust in *you* than in "disciplinary measures."—If either of you need anything else, come over and call me, Melchior. I'll be in my bedroom.

[*Exit.*]

MORITZ: —Your mother means the business with Gretchen.

MELCHIOR: Why, we only spent half a second on it.

MORITZ: Faust himself couldn't have dismissed it more cold-bloodedly!

MELCHIOR: After all, artistically speaking, this outrage isn't the high point of the play. —Suppose Faust just promised to marry the girl and then left her: as I see it he wouldn't be a bit less to blame. As far as I'm concerned, Gretchen could die of a broken heart. —To see the frantic way everyone always fastens on to the subject, you'd think the world revolved around penis and vagina.

MORITZ: To be quite frank, Melchior, since I read your essay, I feel that it does. —It fell at my feet in the first days of the vacation. I had Ploetz's *History* in my hand. —I bolted the door and skimmed throughout the flickering lines as a frightened owl flies through a burning forest. —I think I read most of it with my eyes shut. Your explanations sounded like a series of dim recollections, like a song that one had hummed happily to oneself as a child and then heard on the lips of another as one lay dying. Heartbreaking! —I was most affected by what you wrote about girls. I can't get rid of the impression it made. Believe me, Melchior, to have to suffer wrong is sweeter than to do wrong. To let oneself undergo a sweet wrong undeservedly seems to me the essence of earthly bliss.

MELCHIOR: —I don't want my bliss given to me as charity!

MORITZ: But why not?

MELCHIOR: I don't want anything I haven't had to fight for.

MORITZ: Can you still call that enjoyment, Melchior? –Girls enjoy themselves, Melchior, like the gods in *their* bliss. And a girl's nature is self-protective. A girl keeps herself free of everything bitter till the last moment. She then has the pleasure of seeing all heaven break over her. She hasn't stopped fearing hell when suddenly she notices paradise in full bloom. Her feelings are as fresh as water springing from the rock. She takes up a chalice, a goblet of nectar, which no earthly breath has yet blown upon and – even as is flickers and flares – she drains it! By comparison, a man's satisfaction seems to me shallow, stagnant.

MELCHIOR: Think of it as you like, only keep it to yourself. — I don't like to think about it…

SCENE 2

A living room.

MRS. BERGMANN: [*Her hat on, a shawl around her shoulders and a basket on her arm, enters through the center door with a beaming face.*] Wendla! — Wendla!

WENDLA: [*Appears in her bodice and petticoat at the side door, right.*] What is it, Mother?

MRS. BERGMANN: You're up already, child? —That's a good girl!!

WENDLA: Have you been out already?

MRS. BERGMANN: Be quick and get dressed, you must go down to Ina's. You must take her this basket!

WENDLA: [*Dressing herself completely in the course of what follows.*] You were at Ina's? —How is Ina —still no better?

MRS. BERGMANN: Just think, Wendla, the stork paid Ina a visit last night. Brought her a little boy.

WENDLA: A boy? —A boy! —Oh, that's wonderful! —*That* explains the never-ending "influenza"!

MRS. BERGMANN: A splendid boy!

WENDLA: I must see him, Mother! —So I'm an aunt for the third time—aunt to a girl and two boys!

MRS. BERGMANN: And what boys! —That's what comes of living so near the church! —It's only two years since she went up the altar steps in her muslin dress.

WENDLA: Were you there when the stork brought him?

MRS. BERGMANN: It had just flown away. —Wouldn't you like to pin a rose on your dress?

WENDLA: Why didn't you get there a little sooner, Mother?

MRS. BERGMANN: I think he brought something for you too—a brooch or something.

WENDLA: It's a real shame.

MRS. BERGMANN: But I'm telling you he brought you a brooch!

WENDLA: I have enough brooches...

MRS. BERGMANN: Then be satisfied, child. What else do you want?

WENDLA: I should so terribly like to know whether he flew through the window or down the chimney.

MRS. BERGMANN: You must ask Ina. Uh, huh, you must ask Ina, dear heart. Ina will give you all the details. Ina talked to him a solid half hour.

WENDLA: I shall ask her when I go over.

MRS. BERGMANN: Mind you don't forget, my angel! I should like to know myself whether the stork came through the window or down the chimney.

WENDLA: Or had I better ask the chimney sweep? —The chimney sweep must know best if it comes down the chimney or not.

MRS. BERGMANN: Not the chimney sweep, child! What does he know of the stork? —He'd tell you all sorts of nonsense he doesn't believe himself... Wh-what are you staring at down in the street?

WENDLA: A man, Mother. And he's three times the size of an ox! With feet like steamboats!

MRS. BERGMANN: [*Rushing to the window.*] Impossible! — Impossible!

WENDLA: [*Quickly.*] He's holding a bedstead under his chin and fiddling "The Watch on the Rhine" on it. —Now he's turning the corner...

MRS. BERGMANN: Oh, you're just a big baby still, Wendla. To startle your silly old mother like that ! —Come, take your hat. I'll be surprised if you ever learn sense. —I've given up hope.

WENDLA: So have I, Mother darling. It's sad I haven't learned sense. —Here I have a sister two years married. I myself am an aunt three times over. And I haven't the slightest idea how it all comes about... Don't be angry, Mother darling! Who in the world should I ask but you? Please tell me! Tell me, Mother! Don't scold me for asking. I'm ashamed. Just answer. How does it happen? —You can't seriously expect me to believe in the stork—at fourteen.

MRS. BERGMANN: Good gracious, child, the things you think of! —I really couldn't!

WENDLA: Why not? —It can't be nasty when everyone is so pleased about it.

MRS. BERGMANN: Oh—Oh God preserve me! I'd deserve to be... Go and put on your coat, girl, put on your coat.

WENDLA: I'm going... What if your daughter goes and asks the chimney sweep?

MRS. BERGMANN: It's enough to drive one crazy! —Come, child, come here, I'll tell you! I'll tell you everything... Merciful providence! But not today, Wendla, tomorrow, day after tomorrow, next week. Whenever you like, dear heart...

WENDLA: Today. Now. This minute. —Now that I've seen *you* so upset, *I'm* not likely to calm down.

MRS. BERGMANN: —I can't, Wendla.

WENDLA: Why not? —See, I'll kneel at your feet and put my head in your lap. You can put your apron over my head and talk and talk as if you were alone. I won't flinch, I won't cry out, I'll take what comes!

MRS. BERGMANN: —Heaven knows it's not my fault, Wendla... Well, I'll tell you how you came into the world. —Are you listening, Wendla?

WENDLA: [*Under the apron.*] I'm listening.

[*Pause.*]

MRS. BERGMANN: [*Beside herself.*] —I can't do it. —I couldn't answer for it! —I deserve to be in prison—I deserve to have you taken away from me...

WENDLA: [*Under the apron.*] Courage, Mother!

MRS. BERGMANN: Well then, listen...

WENDLA: [*Under the apron, trembling.*] Oh dear, oh dear!

MRS. BERGMANN: To have a child—you understand what I'm saying, Wendla?

WENDLA: Quick, Mother. I can't bear it!

MRS. BERGMANN: —To have a child—one must love the man— one is married to—love him as only a husband can be loved. One must love him so much, one must love him, Wendla, as you at your age are incapable of loving... Now you know.

WENDLA: [*Getting up.*] God in Heaven!

MRS. BERGMANN: Now you know what trials lie before you!

WENDLA: —And that's all?

MRS. BERGMANN: So help me, God! —And now take the basket and go over to Ina's. You'll get chocolates and cakes there. — Come, let's have another look at you. Laces, boots, silk gloves, sailor blouse, roses in your hair... But that little skirt is definitely too short for you, Wendla.

WENDLA: Have you the meat for dinner, Mother?

MRS. BERGMANN: May the Lord bless you and keep you! — When I have time, I'll put a strip of flouncing on it.

SCENE 3

HÄNSCHEN RILOW, *with a light in his hand, bolts the door behind him and lifts the lid.*

HÄNSCHEN: Hast thou prayed tonight, Desdemona? [*He pulls a reproduction of Palma Vecchio's "Venus" out of his shirt.*] You don't seem to be at your prayers, fair one—contemplatively awaiting whoever might be coming—as in the sweet moment of dawning bliss when I saw you in Jonathan Schlesinger's shop window—these supple limbs are just as beguiling still, the gentle arch of the hips, these firm young breasts—how intoxicated with happiness the great Master must have been when the fourteen-year-old original lay before his very eyes on the sofa!

Will you also visit me in dreams sometimes? — I'll receive you with outstretched arms and kiss you till your breath gives out. You'll take me over like the rightful mistress entering her deserted castle. The gate and all the doors are opened by unseen hands while the fountain joyously begins to plash in the park below.

"It is the cause! — It is the cause" — This frightful pounding in my breast tells you how far from frivolously I murder you. My throat contracts at the thought of my solitary nights. By my soul, child, I swear it is not satiety that sways me! Who would dare boast that he was sated with *you?*

But you suck the marrow from my bones, you crook my back, you steal the light from my young eyes. — Your inhuman modesty makes excessive claims upon me. Your unmoving limbs wear me down. — It was you or I; and the victory is mine.

If I were to count them, the dear departed with whom I have fought the same battle here? "Psyche" by Thumann, another legacy from that dried up Mademoiselle Angélique, rattlesnake in the paradise of my childhood. Correggio's "Io." Lossow's "Galatea." Then a "Cupid" by Bouguereau. "Ada" by J. van Beers — I had to abduct Ada from a secret drawer in father's bureau before I could include her in my harem. A trembling, twitching "Leda" by Makart that I happened on under my brother's school notebooks. Six, O blooming candidate for death, have trod this path to Tartarus before you! Let that be a comfort to you, and do not seek with those looks of supplication to turn my torments to excesses!

You are dying, not for your sins, but for mine. — Only to defend myself from myself do I — with a bleeding heart — commit this seventh wife-murder. Is there not something tragic in the role of Bluebeard? I believe that all his murdered wives together suffered less then he did, strangling any one of them.

But my conscience will rest easier, my body will gain in strength, when you reside no more, you devil, within the red silk cushions of my jewel box. To your place in that voluptuous love-nest I'll admit Bodenhausen's "Lurlei" or Linger's "Forsaken Maiden" or Defregger's "Loni"—they'll help me to recover in short order! Another three months maybe, and your unveiled Jehoshaphat, dear heart, would have begun to eat at my brain as the sun eats butter. This separation of bed and board was overdue.

Phew! There's a Roman Emperor in me, I feel it![6] "She who is about to die salutes thee!"—Girl, girl, why do you press your knees together? —At this late date? —On the threshold of inscrutable eternity? —One twitch, and I'll release you. —One feminine movement, one sign of lust, of sympathy, my girl, and I'll frame you in gold and hang you over my bed! —Have you no inkling that it's only your chastity that drives me to excesses? —Woe unto ye, inhuman ones!

…One never fails to note that she's had an exemplary education. —But then—so have I.

Hast thou prayed tonight, Desdemona?

My heart! I'm having convulsions! —Nonsense! —St. Agnes also died on account of her abstinence, and she wasn't half as naked as you are! —One more kiss on the bloom-

---

6 Wedekind actually names him: Heliogabalus, probably the most disreputable of all the emperors. The "abstinent" 4th century Agnes, named below, was only 13 when she was martyred for saying No to a VIP. (The Venus in this scene is 14.) Another "virgin martyr," Saint Cecilia, is cited three scenes later. Three lines earlier, the reference is to the Book of Joel in the Bible where the Last Judgement is located in the Valley of Jehoshaphat: Hänschen locates this valley between woman's thighs.

ing body, the budding, child's breast, the sweetly rounded—
the cruel knees . . .

It is the cause, it is the cause, my soul.
Let me not name it to you, you chaste stars!
It is the cause! —

[*The picture falls into the depths. He closes the lid.*]

SCENE 4

*A hayloft. —*MELCHIOR *is lying on his back in the new-mown
hay.* WENDLA *climbs the ladder.*

WENDLA: So this is where you've crept off to? —Everyone's looking for you. The wagon has gone out again. You must help.
A thunderstorm is coming up.

MELCHIOR: Keep away! —Keep away from me!

WENDLA: What's the matter with you? —Why are you hiding
your face?

MELCHIOR: Get out of here! —Or I'll throw you down on the
threshing floor!

WENDLA: Now I'm certainly not going.

[*Kneels down beside him.*]

Why don't you come with us to the meadows, Melchior? —
It's dark and stuffy in here. Even if we do get wet to the skin,
what do *we* care!

MELCHIOR: The hay smells so wonderful. —The sky must be as
black as a pall. —All I can see is the poppy gleaming at your
breast—and I can hear your heart beating—

WENDLA: —Don't kiss me, Melchior! —Don't kiss me!

MELCHIOR: —Your heart—I hear it beating—

WENDLA: People love each other—if they kiss - - - - - - don't, don't - - - - - -

MELCHIOR: There is no such thing as love! That's a fact. —It's all just selfishness and self-seeking. —I love you as little as you love me. —

WENDLA: —Don't - - - - - - Don't, Melchior! - - - - - -

MELCHIOR: - - - - - - Wendla!

WENDLA: Oh, Melchior! - - - - -don't - - - - - - - - - - -don't - - - - - - - - - - - - - - - - -don't - - - - - - - - - - -don't
- -

SCENE 5

MRS. GABOR, *seated, writing.*

MRS. GABOR:

Dear Mr. Stiefel,

Having for twenty-four hours considered and reconsidered all that you have written to me, I take up my pen with a heavy heart. I am unable, I give you my sacred word on it, to provide you with the cost of a passage to America. I have not so much money at my disposal, and even if I had, it would be the greatest conceivable sin to place in your hand the means of acting on a sudden whim so grave in its consequences. You would do me a bitter injustice, Mr. Stiefel, if you were to attribute this refusal to lack of love. On the other hand, it would be the most brutal violation of my duty as a motherly friend were I to let myself be persuaded by your temporary loss of control into losing my own head and blindly following my own first impulse. Should you wish it,

I will gladly write to your parents. I will try to convince them that in the course of the term you have done all you could. You have so used up your strength—I shall point out—that a strict judgment on your failure would be not only unjustifiable but in the highest degree prejudicial to your mental and physical health.

Frankly, Mr. Stiefel, your veiled threats to take your own life, should you be refused the means of escape, have slightly alienated my sympathies. Let a misfortune be never so undeserved, one should not permit oneself to be driven to forbidden measures. The way in which you seek to make me, who have never shown you anything but good will, responsible for a possible dreadful misdeed on your part could all too easily be interpreted by the hostile as attempted blackmail. I must confess that such behavior in you, who otherwise seem so aware of your duty to yourself, is the last thing I would have expected. Meanwhile, I am firmly convinced that you were too much under the influence of the initial fright to be fully aware of what you were doing.

And so I confidently hope that these words of mine will find you already in a more controlled frame of mind. Accept the matter as it stands. In my opinion, it is quite impermissible to judge a young man by his school reports. We have too many examples of very bad students making splendid people, and on the other hand of excellent students acquitting themselves indifferently in life. At all events, I give you my assurance that, as far as it lies in my power, your failure shall change nothing in your relationship with Melchior. It will always be a pleasure to me to see my son associating with a young man who, however the world may judge him, has been able to win my fullest sympathy.

So chin up, Mr. Stiefel! —Such crises of one kind or another confront each of us and must be overcome. If everyone had recourse to poison or the dagger there would soon be no human beings left in the world. Let me hear from you again soon. With warmest greetings from your still devoted motherly friend,

Fanny G.

SCENE 6

The Bergmanns' garden in the morning sunlight.

WENDLA: Why did you slip out of the room? —To look for violets! —Because Mother can see me smiling. - - Why can't you keep your lips together? —I don't know. —I really don't know, I can't find the words...

The path is like a plush carpet—not a pebble, not a thorn. —My feet don't touch the ground... Oh, how sweetly I slept last night!

This is where they were. —I feel as solemn as a nun at Communion. —Sweet violets! —All right, Mother dear, I'm ready now for the penitential robe. —Oh God, if only someone would come that I could embrace, that I could tell the whole story to!

SCENE 7

Dusk. The sky is slightly overcast. The path winds through low brush and reeds. From a little distance the murmur of the river can be heard.

MORITZ: It's better this way. —I don't belong. Let the rest of them knock their heads together. —I'll close the door behind me and step out in the open. —Pay for the privilege of being kicked around? I never pushed before. Why now? —I've signed no contract with the Almighty. People will make of this what they want. I've been driven to it. —I don't hold my parents responsible. All the same they must have been prepared for the worst. They were old enough to know what they were doing. I was an infant when I came into the world, or no doubt I'd have been smart enough to become someone else. —Why should I suffer because everyone else was already there?

One would have to be a perfect fool... if someone makes me a present of a mad dog I give him his mad dog back, well, I'm human, and...

One would have to be a perfect fool.

One is born entirely by chance. And if, after mature consideration—oh, it's enough to make one want to shoot oneself!

—At least the weather's being considerate. It's been looking like rain all day, but it's kept fine after all. - - An unusual peace reigns. In all Nature, not a discordant note. Earth and sky—one transparent cobweb. Everything feeling fine. The whole landscape's sweet as a lullaby. "Sleep, princeling, sleep," as Fräulein Snandulia sang. Pity she holds her elbows so ungracefully. —The last time I danced was at the party on St. Cecilia's day. Fräulein Snandulia only dances with "eligible" men. Her silk dress was cut low back and front. Down to her belt behind and, in front, so low you could almost pass out. —She couldn't have been wearing a slip...

- -

That[7] might be something that could still hold me. — More for curiosity's sake. —It must be an extraordinary sensation—it must feel like being swept away by a torrent—I

---

7 The word "that" presumably refers back to the preceding line of dashes. Here and elsewhere in this script, Wedekind sprays dashes (and sometimes block capitals) to suggest what words don't say. Often, as here, that is some form of sexual excitement. Has Moritz had an orgasm at this point? Or just an erection? "It" in the next sentence-but-one clearly is sexual intercourse: for him "the job not done."

won't tell anyone I've returned with the job not done. I shall act as if I've taken part... There's something to be ashamed of in having been human without getting to know the most human thing of all. — You were in Egypt, dear sir, and did not see the Pyramids? —

I mustn't cry again today. I mustn't think of my funeral. — Melchior will put a wreath on my coffin. Pastor Skinnytum will condole with my parents. Rektor Sunstroke will cite examples from history. — I don't suppose they'll give me a gravestone. I'd have liked a snow-white marble urn on a column of black granite, but, I won't miss it. Memorials are for the living.

I'd need a year to say good-by to everyone in my thoughts.

I mustn't cry again. I'm glad to be able to look back without bitterness. How many happy evenings I've spent with Melchior! —under the willows on the riverbank; at the keeper's cottage; out on the military highway where the five lindens are; on the hillside among the peaceful ruins of the castle. — When the time comes, I'll think as hard as I can of whipped cream. It won't hold me up, but it's filling, the aftertaste is pleasant...And I thought human beings were a lot worse too. Never found one that wouldn't have wished to do his best. I pitied many — on my own account.

I proceed to the altar like that kid in ancient Etruria: his death rattle purchased his brothers' good fortune. — I savor the mysterious terrors of parting, drop by drop. I sob with grief at this my destiny. — Life has given me the cold shoulder. From the other side, kind, grave faces beckon: the headless queen, the headless queen — sympathy awaits me with soft arms... "Thou Shalt Not..." Shalt not what? Your commandments, my dears, are for children. Myself, I have a complimentary ticket to the next world. If one puts down the cup, off flies the butterfly, and the mirage stops giving trouble. —But why must you all play fast and loose with the deception? —The mists dissolve. Life is a matter of taste.

ILSE: [*Her clothes torn, a colored kerchief on her head, grabs him by the shoulder from behind.*] What have you lost?

MORITZ: Ilse!

ILSE: What are you looking for *here*?

MORITZ: Why did you give me such a fright?

ILSE: What are you looking for? —What have you lost?

MORITZ: Why frighten me so dreadfully?

ILSE: I've come from the town. I'm going home.

MORITZ: I don't know what I've lost.

ILSE: Then looking for it won't help.

MORITZ: Hell, hell, hell!

ILSE: I haven't been home in four days.

MORITZ: —And quiet as a cat!

ILSE: Because I'm wearing my ballet slippers. —Mother's eyes will pop when she sees me. —Come with me as far as our house!

MORITZ: Where've you been, by the way?

ILSE: Where Priapus reigns.

MORITZ: Priapus?

ILSE: At Nohl's, Fehrendorf's, Padinsky's, Lenz's, Rank's, Spühler's—everybody. Will she be mad? Wow!

MORITZ: Are they painting you?

ILSE: Fehrendorf is painting me as a saint on a pillar. I stand on a Corinthian column. Fehrendorf is a real nut, let me tell you. Last time I trod on one of his tubes of paint. So he wipes his brush in my hair. I give him a whack on the ear. He throws his palette at my head. I upset his easel. He comes after me with this mahlstick, over sofas, tables, chairs, all around the studio. Behind the stove I find a sketch. "Be good, or I tear it up!"—He called a truce and in the end kisses me something terrible.

MORITZ: Where did you spend the night in town?

ILSE: Yesterday at Nohl's—day before yesterday Boyokevich's—Sunday at Oikonomopulos's. At Padinsky's there was champagne. Valabregez had sold his "Sick with the Plague." Adolar drank from the ash tray. Lenz sang "She murdered her child,"[8] and Adolar played the guitar to shreds. I was so drunk they had to carry me to bed. —You still going to school, Moritz?

MORITZ: No, no . . . I'm leaving this term.

ILSE: Quite right, too. Goodness, how time flies when you're earning a living! Remember how we used to play robbers—Wendla Bergmann and you and me and the others? You'd come over in the evening and drink milk fresh from the goat? —What's Wendla doing? I saw her lately watching the floods. —What's Melchi Gabor doing? —Does he still look so solemn? —We used to stand opposite each other in singing lesson.

MORITZ: He philosophizes.

ILSE: Wendla came over and brought Mother some jam. I was sitting for Isidore Landauer that day. As Holy Mary, Mother of God, with the infant Jesus. He's an idiot. Disgusting, too. Ugh, like a weather-cock! —D'you have a hang-over?

MORITZ: From last night! —We soused like hippopotami. I came reeling home about five o'clock.

8 A Schiller poem.

ILSE: Just look at you. —Any girls there?

MORITZ: Arabella, beer-nymph of Andalusia! —The landlord left us alone with her all night . . .

ILSE: Just look at you, Moritz! —I never had a hang-over in my life. At the last Carnival I didn't go to bed or take my clothes off for three days and three nights. From the ball to the café, afternoons to the Bellavista, evenings to the cabaret, nights to the ball again. Lena was there, and fat Viola. —The third night Heinrich found me.

MORITZ: Was he looking for you?

ILSE: He stumbled over my arm. I'd passed out in the snow on the street. —Then I moved in with him. Didn't leave for fourteen days—a terrible time! Mornings, had to put on his Persian bathrobe. Evenings, had to walk the room in a black page outfit—white lace at the neck, knees, and sleeves. Every day he photographed me in a different pose—once on the arm of the sofa as Ariadne, once as Leda, once on all fours as a female Nebuchadnezzar. And all the time he raved about killing, shooting, suicide, gas fumes. In the early morning he'd bring a pistol into bed, fill it with cartridges, and stick it into my chest. "Wink just once, and I fire!"—Oh, and he would have fired, Moritz, he would have! —Then he'd put the thing in his mouth like a blowpipe. To awaken my self preservation instincts! After which—brrr—he'd have put a bullet through my spine.

MORITZ: Is Heinrich still alive?

ILSE: How'd I know? —There was a mirror in the ceiling over the bed. Made the little room seem high as a tower and brilliant as an opera house. There you are, large as life, hanging down from the sky! At night I had ghastly dreams. God, O God, would day ever come? —"Good night, Ilse. When you're asleep, you look lovely for murdering!"

MORITZ: Is this Heinrich still alive?

ILSE: I hope to God not! —One day while he was getting some absinthe I threw my coat around me and crept out onto the street. The Carnival was over. The police pick me up and ask me what I'm doing in men's clothes. They take me to the station. Then Nohl came, and Fehrendorf, Padinsky, Spühler, Oikonomopulos, the whole Priapia! They bailed me out. Transported me in a cab to Adolar's studio. Since then I've been faithful to the gang. Fehrendorf is an ape, Nohl is a pig, Boyokevich an owl, Loison a hyena, Oikonomopulos a camel, yet I love them one and all and wouldn't want to be tied to anyone else if the world was full of archangels and millionaires!

MORITZ: —I must go back, Ilse.

ILSE: Come as far as our house!

MORITZ: —What for ? —What for? —

ILSE: To drink warm goat's milk. —I'll curl your hair for you and hang a little bell round your neck. —And we still have a rocking horse you can play with.

MORITZ: I must go back. —I've still got the Sassanids, the Sermon on the Mount, and the parallelepipedon on my conscience. —Good night, Ilse!

ILSE: Sweet dreams!... D'you all still go out to the wigwam where Melchi Gabor buried my tomahawk? —Brrr! By the time any of you are ready, I'll be on the rubbish heap.

[*Rushes away.*]

MORITZ: [*Alone.*] —A single word would have done it. — [*He shouts.*] —Ilse! —Ilse! —Thank God she can't hear now.

— I'm not in the mood. — You have to have a clear head and feel good. — A pity to miss such a chance, though, a great pity!

…I'll say I had great crystal mirrors over my bed — trained an unruly filly — made her strut across the carpet before me in long, black, silk stockings and black patent-leather shoes and long, black, kid gloves and black velvet round her neck —stifled her with my pillow in a sudden attack of madness… when the talk is of lust I shall smile…I shall — SCREAM! I SHALL SCREAM! — TO BE YOU, ILSE! — WHERE PRIAPUS REIGNS! — UNCONSCIOUSNESS! — IT SAPS MY STRENGTH! — THIS CHILD OF FORTUNE, CHILD OF SUNSHINE, DAUGHTER OF JOY UPON MY WAY OF SORROWS! — OH! — OH!

— —
— —

[*In the bushes on the riverbank.*] How did I get back here? That grassy bank. The king's tapers[9] seem to have grown since yesterday. The view through the willows is the same, though. — How sluggish the river is —like molten lead. —Don't let me forget… [*He takes* MRS. GABOR*'s letter from his pocket and burns it.*] — Look at those sparks! "In and out and roundabout!" — Ghosts! — Shooting stars! —

Before I lit that match, you could still see the grass and a strip of light on the horizon. —It's got dark now. I won't go home again now.

---

9 I have used this rarer name for Great Mulleins because it is so precise and equivalent of the German *Königskerzen* and preserves the sexual connotations here and at the end of Act Three, Scene 2. Priapus presides over this whole episode.

ACT III

SCENE 1

Faculty Room. —Portraits of Pestalozzi and J. J. Rousseau on the walls.[10] *Around the green table over which several gas lamps are burning sit* PROFESSORS CALFLOVE, THICKSTICK, STARVELING, BONEBREAKER, STICKYTONGUE, *and* FLYKILLER. *At the head of the table on a raised chair,* REKTOR SUNSTROKE. CATCHEMQUICK, *the porter, cowers by the door.*

SUNSTROKE: . . . Have any of you gentlemen further remarks to make? —Gentlemen—if we have no alternative but to apply to the Ministry of Education for the expulsion of this delinquent student, it is for weighty reasons. We must atone for the evil which has already befallen, and equally we must protect this institution against similar calamities in the future. We must chastise this delinquent student for the demoralizing influence he has exercised upon his classmates; and above all we must prevent him from exercising such influence upon his classmates. We have the duty to protect this institution from the ravages of a suicide epidemic which has already broken out in various other schools, and which has set at nought all efforts to teach the boys the obligations of an educated existence. —Have any of you gentlemen further remarks to make?

THICKSTICK: I can no longer resist the conclusion that the time has come at last to open a window somewhere.

STICKYTONGUE: The a-a-atmosphere which p-prevails here resembles that of underground ca-ca-ca-catacombs, or the archives of the lawcourts in old Wetzlar.

---

10 Symbols of exactly the opposite kind of education to that which this school is offering.

SUNSTROKE: Catchemquick!

CATCHEMQUICK: Yes, Herr Rektor?

SUNSTROKE: Open a window! There is atmosphere enough outside, thank God. —Have any of you gentlemen further remarks to make?

FLYKILLER: If my colleagues wish to have a window open I have nothing against it. All I ask is that it should not be the window immediately behind my back.

SUNSTROKE: Catchemquick!

CATCHEMQUICK: Yes, Herr Rektor?

SUNSTROKE: Open the other window! —Have any of you gentlemen further remarks to make?

STARVELING: Without wishing to contradict our Rektor, I should like to remind him of the fact that the other window has been bricked up since last autumn.

SUNSTROKE: Catchemquick!

CATCHEMQUICK: Yes, Herr Rektor?

SUNSTROKE: Let the other window remain closed! I feel compelled, gentlemen, to put the matter to a vote. May I ask those who are *for* the opening of the only window in question to rise? [*He counts.*] —One, two, three. —One, two, three. —Catchemquick!

CATCHEMQUICK: Yes, Herr Rektor?

SUNSTROKE: Let window number one likewise remain closed. —I for my part am convinced that the prevailing atmosphere leaves nothing to be desired. —Have any of you gentlemen further remarks to make? —Gentlemen! —Should we fail to apply to the Ministry of Education for the expulsion of this delinquent student, the Ministry of Education will hold *us* responsible for the misfortune which has descended upon us. Of the various schools, afflicted with suicide epidemics, those at which twenty-five per cent of the students have fallen victim to the epidemic have been suspended by the Ministry of Education. It is our duty as custodians of this institution to protect it from such a shattering blow. We are in no position to regard the other qualifications of the delinquent student as mitigating circumstances. While a lenient procedure might be justifiable in respect of the delinquent student, in respect of this institution, endangered as it is in the most serious way, it would *not* be justifiable. We find ourselves under the necessity of judging the guilty lest we, the innocent, should ourselves be judged. —Catchemquick!

CATCHEMQUICK: Yes, Herr Rektor?

SUNSTROKE: Bring him up!

[*Exit* CATCHEMQUICK.]

STICKYTONGUE: If the p-prevailing a-a-atmosphere is authoritatively regarded as leaving little or nothing to be desired, I would like to propose that during the s-summer vacation the other window be b-b-b-b-b-b-bricked up!

FLYKILLER: If our colleague Stickytongue considers our premises to be inadequately ventilated I should like to propose that our colleague Stickytongue have a ventilator installed in his frontal cavity.

STICKYTONGUE: I d-d-don't have to put up with that sort of thing! I d-d-don't have to put up with insolence! —I am master of my f-f-f-f-five senses!

SUNSTROKE: I must ask our colleagues Flykiller and Stickytongue to observe a measure of decorum. The delinquent student would seem to be already on the threshold.

[CATCHEMQUICK *opens the door and* MELCHIOR, *pale but composed, steps before the assembly.*]

SUNSTROKE: Come nearer the table! —After Rentier Stiefel had been informed of his son Moritz's impious misdeed, the bewildered father searched his son Moritz's effects in the hope of learning thereby the occasion of this loathsome crime. He thus chanced, in a place which has no bearing upon the matter in hand, on a document which, without entirely explaining the loathsome crime, nevertheless provides an all too adequate explanation of the criminal's morally deranged predisposition. The document in question is a treatise twenty pages long in dialogue form, entitled *Copulation*, equipped with life-size illustrations and teeming with shameless indecencies, a document that would meet the most extravagant demands of an abandoned libertine, a connoisseur in pornographic literature. —

MELCHIOR: I . . .

SUNSTROKE: Please hold your tongue! —As soon as Rentier Stiefel had handed over the document in question and we had promised the bewildered father to make the author known to him at any cost, the handwriting was compared with the handwriting of all the fellow students of the impious deceased, and in the unanimous judgment of the entire teaching staff, as well as in the expert opinion of our respected colleague in calligraphy, it betrayed the profoundest similarity to your own. —

MELCHIOR: I . . .

SUNSTROKE: Please hold your tongue! —Regardless of the overwhelming fact of such a resemblance, recognized, as it is, by unimpeachable authorities, we feel ourselves entitled to abstain for the time being from taking action in order to interrogate the culprit on the crime against decency with which he is charged and on the impulse to self-destruction which arose therefrom. —

MELCHIOR: I...

SUNSTROKE: You are to answer the precisely formulated questions which I am about to put to you one by one with a simple and unassuming "yes" or "no."—Catchemquick!

CATCHEMQUICK: Yes, Herr Rektor?

SUNSTROKE: The dossier! —I must ask the secretary, Professor Flykiller, to transcribe the proceedings, as far as possible word for word, from this point on. [*To* MELCHIOR.] Are you familiar with this document?

MELCHIOR: Yes.

SUNSTROKE: Do you know what this document contains?

MELCHIOR: Yes.

SUNSTROKE: Is the handwriting of this document yours?

MELCHIOR: Yes.

STICKYTONGUE: B-b-but you might as well make the b b-boy[11] responsible for b-b-being b-b-born! Gave serious th-th-thought to serious series of events, wrote seriously about them! Had the m-m-makings of a N-na-natural Scientist!

FLYKILLER: I am a Natural Scientist and I have NEVER written about such a series of events!

STICKYTONGUE: I f-f-feel compelled to st-st-state that the lad is g-g-going through a tr-tr-transition during which N-n-nature f-f-forces such m-m-matters into the foreground!

---

11 Stickytongue's interjection here and Flykiller's contention with him are in Wedekind's 1894 text but not in the now standard text. But they are an integral part of the play, thematically speaking. CF. the Hänschen Rilow episodes. And Act 3, Scene 4.

FLYKILLER: YOU need to have the frontal cavity of your cerebrum drained!

STICKYTONGUE: When you and I were t-t-together in s-s-school you made counterfeit money which l-l-later you s-s-stole from the b-b-boys' p-p-pockets!

FLYKILLER: Onanism! That's what YOU did! O—

SUNSTROKE: Oh! Oh!

CALFLOVE: Oh! Oh! Oh!

ALL TOGETHER: Oh!

STICKYTONGUE: Which of us didn't?

MELCHIOR: I...

SUNSTROKE: Please hold your tongue! Was the indecent document born in your brain?

MELCHIOR: Yes. —Please point out to me one indecency, Herr Rektor.

SUNSTROKE: You are to answer the precisely formulated questions which I put to you with a simple and unassuming "yes" or "no."

MELCHIOR: What I wrote is fact, no more, no less. Facts well known to you.

SUNSTROKE: Scoundrel!!

MELCHIOR: Please show me one offense against morals in the document.

SUNSTROKE: Do you imagine I shall let myself be made a clown of by you? —Catchemquick...!

MELCHIOR: I...

SUNSTROKE: You have as little respect for the dignity of your assembled teachers as you have sense of decency! You are flouting the instinctive human feeling for modesty and discretion! You are flouting the moral order itself! —Catchemquick!

CATCHEMQUICK: [*Placing a document before him.*] Here, Herr Rektor.

SUNSTROKE: Such language! [*Taking the document up.*] This is Langenscheidt's *Agglutinative Worldspeak in Three Hours!*

MELCHIOR: I . . .

SUNSTROKE: I call upon the secretary, Professor Flykiller, to close the minutes!

MELCHIOR: I . . .

SUNSTROKE: Please hold your tongue! —Catchemquick!

CATCHEMQUICK: Yes, Herr Rektor?

SUNSTROKE: Take him downstairs!

SCENE 2

A cemetery in streaming rain. PASTOR SKINNYTUM *stands before an open grave, with his umbrella up. On his right* REN-TIER STIEFEL *and the latter's friend,* GOATMILKER, *and* UNCLE PROBST. *On his left* REKTOR SUNSTROKE *and* PROFESSOR BONE-BREAKER. *Boys from the school complete the circle. At a little distance* MARTHA *and* ILSE, *by a half-ruined gravestone.*

PASTOR SKINNYTUM: —He who has lived and worked for evil in self-willed carnal denial of the honor which is God's due shall die the death of the body! —But he who lightly casts from him the cross which the All-merciful has laid upon him for his sins, verily, verily I say unto you, he shall die an *eternal* death! — [*He throws a spadeful of earth into the grave.*] Let us who dutifully tread the path of thorns praise the Lord, the All-bountiful, and thank Him for the inscrutable disposition of His grace. For as surely as this person died a threefold death, as surely will our Lord God lead the righteous to everlasting life. —Amen.

RENTIER STIEFEL: [*His voice strangled with sobs, throws a spadeful of earth into the grave.*] The boy was no son of mine! —The boy was no son of mine! —I never liked him—from the beginning.

REKTOR SUNSTROKE: [*Throws a spadeful of earth into the grave.*] Suicide, as the weightiest transgression against the moral order, is the weightiest proof of the existence of the moral order, in that the suicide, by saving the moral order the necessity of passing judgment, *ipso facto* confirms the existence of the moral order.

PROFESSOR BONEBREAKER: [*Throws a spadeful of earth into the grave.*] Debased, deformed, debauched, depraved, and degenerate!

UNCLE PROBST: [*Throws a spadeful of earth into the grave.*] I wouldn't have believed my own mother if she'd told me a child could treat his parents so basely!

FRIEND GOATMILKER: [*Throws a spadeful of earth into the grave.*] Could treat a father thus who for more than twenty years, early and late, had entertained no thought but the welfare of his child!

PASTOR SKINNYTUM: [*Pressing* RENTIER STIEFEL'*s hand.*] We know that all things work together for good to them that love God. I Corinthians 12:15[12] Think of the disconsolate mother, and seek to replace what she has lost with love redoubled. —

---

12 Actually, this is Romans 8:28. But Skinnytum knows, it seems, what I Corinthians Chapter 12 does say about the human body and the importance of what are considered its weak spots.

REKTOR SUNSTROKE: [*Pressing* RENTIER STIEFEL*'s hand.*] We'd probably have been unable to give him his promotion in any case.

PROFESSOR BONEBREAKER: [*Pressing* RENTIER STIEFEL*'s hand.*] And if we *had* given him the promotion he'd have flunked out next spring sure enough!

UNCLE PROBST: [*Pressing* RENTIER STIEFEL*'s hand.*] Above all, your duty now is to think of yourself. You are a pater familias ...!

FRIEND GOATMILKER: [*Pressing* RENTIER STIEFEL*'s hand.*] Entrust yourself to my guidance! —Wretched weather, enough to make the bowels quake! —If you don't sit back with a hot grog, and quick, it gets you right in the heart!

RENTIER STIEFEL: [*Blowing his nose.*] The boy was no son of mine ... the boy was no son of mine ...

[*Exit* RENTIER STIEFEL, *accompanied by* PASTOR SKINNY-TUM, REKTOR SUNSTROKE, PROFESSOR BONEBREAKER, UNCLE PROBST *and* FRIEND GOATMILKER. *The rain abates.*]

HÄNSCHEN RILOW: [*Throws a spadeful of earth into the grave.*] Rest in peace, honest fellow! —Give my greetings to my everlasting brides of sacrificial memory and commend me most devotedly to God in all His grace, O Simple Simon! —I daresay they'll put a scarecrow on your grave in memory of your angelic simplicity ...

GEORG: Has the pistol been found?

ROBERT: No need to look for any pistol!

ERNST: Did you see him, Robert?

ROBERT: It's a damned fraud! —Who saw him? —Who?

OTTO: That's just it: they'd thrown a sheet over him.

GEORG: Was his tongue hanging out?

ROBERT: His eyes! —That was why they'd put the sheet over him.

OTTO: Horrible!

HÄNSCHEN RILOW: [*To* ROBERT.] Are you positive he hanged himself?

ERNST: They say he had no head left at all.

OTTO: Nonsense! —Rubbish!

ROBERT: I had the rope in my hands! —I've never seen a hanged man yet who didn't have to be covered up.

GEORG: He couldn't have taken himself off in a nastier way!

HÄNSCHEN RILOW: Hell, do you expect hanging to be pretty?

OTTO: Matter of fact, he owes me five marks. We made a bet. He swore he could keep his place.

HÄNSCHEN RILOW: It's your fault he's where he is. You called him a show-off.

OTTO: Bosh! I have to grind all night, too, If he'd done his Greek Lit. he wouldn't have needed to hang himself.

ERNST: Done your essay, Otto?

OTTO: Only the introduction.

ERNST: I can't think what to say.

GEORG: Weren't you there when Calflove assigned it?

HÄNSCHEN RILOW: I shall fix myself up with something out of Democritus.

ERNST: I'll see if I can find something in Meyer's *Lexicon*.

OTTO: Have you done the Virgil for tomorrow? —

[*The Schoolboys leave.* —MARTHA *and* ILSE *approach the grave.*]

ILSE: Quick, quick! —The gravediggers are coming.

MARTHA: Wouldn't it be better if we waited with the flowers, Ilse?

ILSE: What for? —We can bring fresh ones. Fresh ones and then more fresh ones. —There are plenty more anemones where these came from.

MARTHA: You're right, Ilse! —

[*She throws a wreath of ivy into the grave,* ILSE *opens her apron and lets fall a profusion of fresh anemones*[13] *on the coffin.*]

MARTHA: I shall dig up our roses. I'll get beaten in any case. — Here they'll really grow!

ILSE: I'll water them whenever I come by. I'll bring forget-me-nots from the brook, and irises from home.

MARTHA: It will be a glorious display! Glorious!

ILSE: I was just across the bridge there when I heard the shot.

MARTHA: Poor kid.

ILSE: And I know why he did it too, Martha.

MARTHA: Did he say something?

ILSE: "Parallelepipedon!" But don't tell anyone.

MARTHA: Cross my heart!

ILSE: —Here's the pistol.

---

13 The contorted Christianity of the grown-ups is followed by the pure paganism of Ilse and the children. Anemones flowed from the blood of the dying Adonis, and already in Act II, Scene 7 there had been a hint of Venus–Ilse, Adonis=Moritz.

MARTHA: So that's why no one could find it.

ILSE: I took it out of his hand when I came by next morning.

MARTHA: Give it to me, Ilse! —Please give it to me!

ILSE: No. I'll keep it as a souvenir.

MARTHA: Ilse, is it true he's in there without a head?

ILSE: He must have loaded it with water. —The king's-tapers were sprinkled all over with blood. His brains were hanging from the willow branches.

SCENE 3

MR. *and* MRS. GABOR.

MRS. GABOR: ... They needed a scapegoat. They couldn't allow these spreading accusations to fall on themselves. So now that my child has had the misfortune to fall foul of these fogies at the right moment, I, his own mother, am supposed to finish the hangmen's work for them? —Heaven forbid!

MR. GABOR: —For fourteen years I have observed in silence your "intelligent" methods of bringing up children. They were at variance with *my* ideas. My own conviction has always been that a child is not a plaything, that a child is entitled to our most solemn and serious attention, but I told myself that if the charm and intelligence of one parent *could* replace the serious principles of the other, then, possibly, they might deserve to do so. —I'm not reproaching you, Fanny, but do not stand in my way when I seek to make good the wrong that you and I have done our boy!

MRS. GABOR: I shall stand in your way as long as there's a drop of warm blood in my veins! My boy will be lost in a Reformatory. A criminal nature might be improved in such a place, I don't know. I do know this: a good boy would only be turned into a criminal by such a place —as surely as a plant dies without sun and air. I'm not aware of having done wrong. Today, as always, I thank Heaven for having shown me the way to give my child an upright character and a noble mind. What has he done that's so terrible? — It would not occur to me to try to excuse a fault —but it wasn't his fault they turned him out of school. Even if it *was*, he's atoned for it. Maybe you understand all this better than I do. Theoretically you may be right. But I can't let my only child be hounded to death!

MR. GABOR: That doesn't depend on us, Fanny. — It's a risk we have accepted, just like our happiness. Whoever's not strong enough for the march falls by the wayside. And it isn't the worst thing, after all, if what's inevitable comes in good time. Leave it to Heaven to protect us from it! Our duty is to strengthen the weak of will as long as reason can find a way.

— "It's not his fault he was thrown out of school." If he had *not* been thrown out, that wouldn't have been his fault either, I suppose. — You were too lighthearted. You only see childish naughtiness when it's a case of a fundamental flaw in the character. You women are not qualified to judge of such matters. Anyone who could write what Melchior wrote must be rotten to the core; the very marrow is affected; a halfway healthy nature would be incapable of such a thing. None of us are saints, each one of us strays from the straight and narrow path, but there's a principle involved. This was no unintentional lapse, but the documentation, with horrifying clarity, of a purpose openly entertained, a natural drive toward immorality for its own sake. This piece of writing is evidence of that extreme degree of spiritual corruption which we clinicians describe as "moral   depravity."   —   Whether   anything can be done for such a state of mind I cannot say, but if we are to keep alive the last ray of hope, if we are to keep our consciences as parents of the person in question unstained, it is time to take a stand. —Let's not go on quarreling, Fanny. I know how hard it will be for you. I know you idolize him because your own great gifts are mirrored in his. Be stronger than yourself. Show yourself selfless for once where your son is concerned!

MRS. GABOR: It takes a man to talk like that! It takes a man to let himself be fooled by dead words! It takes a man to see no further than his nose this way! —Melchior has always been impressionable, I saw that from the start, and acted according to my conscience and my best judgment. But, are we responsible for accidents? Suppose a tile falls on your head and a friend of yours—your father, say—walks all over you instead of tending your wounds? —I'll not see my child murdered before my very eyes. What is a mother for? — That he should write such things—doesn't it prove how utterly artless he is, how childlike, how stupid, how innocent? To find moral corruption here, one must have the soul of a bureaucrat, one must be wholly ignorant of human nature, one must... Say what you want. If you put Melchior in a Reformatory, it is over between us. Then let me see if— somewhere in the world—I can't find a way to snatch my son from his destruction!

MR. GABOR: You'll have to resign yourself to it—if not today, tomorrow. Coming to terms with misfortune isn't easy for anyone. I'll be at your side. If your courage threatens to give out, I'll do everything in my power to comfort you. The future looks so gray and overcast. If I lost you too, it would be the end.

MRS. GABOR: Never to see him again! Never again! He can't stand crudity, he'll never get used to the filth of it, he'll cut himself

loose —with the ghastly example of Moritz always before him!
—And if I see him again —the joy of spring in his heart —his
bright laughter —everything about him —his child's determi-
nation to fight for the right and the good —oh, his heart was
pure and clear as the morning sky —it was my most precious
possession...If there's an injustice here that cries out for expi-
ation, turn against me, do what you like with me, I'll take the
blame, but keep your frightful hands off my child!

MR. GABOR: He has gone wrong.

MRS. GABOR: He has not gone wrong!

MR. GABOR: He has gone wrong!! —I'd have given anything to
spare you this, I know how you love him. —This morning a
woman came to see me. She was beside herself. She could hardly speak. She held this letter in her hand. It's addressed to her fifteen-year-old daughter. She told me she'd opened it out of
foolish curiosity, the girls not being home. In this letter Melchior
tells the fifteen-year-old child that what he's done is leaving
him not peace, he has sinned against her, et cetera, et cetera,
but that naturally he'll answer for everything, she mustn't take it
to heart even if there are consequences, he's already taking steps
to help her, his expulsion will make things easier, what was an
error at the time may yet turn out for the best —and a lot more.

MRS. GABOR: Impossible!

MR. GABOR: The letter's a forgery. A deception. His expulsion is the
talk of the town, and someone's trying to build on that. I
haven't spoken yet with the boy —but look at the handwriting!
The style!

MRS. GABOR: What a rotten, shameless trick!

MR. GABOR: I'm afraid you're right.

[*Pause.*]

MRS. GABOR: No, No! Never![14]

MR. GABOR: It'll be better for us. —The woman wrung her hands and asked me what she should do. I suggested she might stop her fifteen-year-old daughter from hanging around haylofts. Luckily she left her letter with me. —If we now send Melchior to another school where he's not even under parental supervision, we'll have a repetition of the same case in three weeks: another expulsion—he'll make a habit of it—the "joy of spring" can be lasting. —So what should I do with the boy, Fanny? Tell me.

MRS. GABOR: The Reformatory.

MR. GABOR: The...?

MRS. GABOR: Reformatory.

MR. GABOR: Where he will find what was wrongly withheld from him: iron discipline, principles, and a moral compulsion to which he must in all circumstances submit. —A Reformatory isn't the abode of horror that you imagine: the emphasis is on developing Christian thoughts and Christian feelings. The boy will learn to desire the good, not just the interesting. As for conduct, he will learn to ask what is lawful, not just what is natural. —Half an hour ago I got a letter from my brother confirming this woman's statement: Melchior confided in him and asked for 200 marks to flee to England...

MRS. GABOR: [*Covering her face.*] Merciful heaven.

---

14 A very strong Reversal, but what exactly brings it about? Not the discovery of the "shameless trick" performed by an unknown forger-trouble-maker but, rather, the realization (albeit based on a forgery) that Melchior, committed a larger "sin" than writing an essay On Copulation, and that People (albeit forgers) know about this. Since, however, the Gabors have the letter, they can hold on to it, and remove Melchior from the local scene. Two Removals dominate this part of the plot: that of Melchior and that, of course, of Wendla's offspring.

SCENE 4

Reformatory—a corridor. —DIETHELM, REINHOLD, RUPRECHT, HELMUTH, GASTON, *and* MELCHIOR.

DIETHELM: Here's a twenty-pfenning piece.

REINHOLD: What of it?

DIETHELM: I put it on the floor. You all stand round it in a circle. The one that hits it first, gets it.

RUPRECHT: Aren't you joining in, Melchior?

MELCHIOR: No, thank you.

HELMUTH: The Joseph![15]

GASTON: He couldn't, oh, no! He's here for a vacation!

MELCHIOR: [*To himself.*] It's not smart for me to stay out. They all watch me. I'll have to join in. You crack up if you don't. —They're killing themselves, that's what prison's done for them. —If I break my neck, good. If I make a getaway, also good. I can't lose. —Ruprecht is getting to be my friend. He knows the ropes here. —I'll reward him with the story of Tamar, daughter-in-law of Judah, Moab, Lot and his daughters, Queen Vashti, Abishag the Shunammite . . . He has the sorriest face in the outfit.

RUPRECHT: I've got it.

HELMUTH: Here *I* come!

GASTON: Day after tomorrow maybe.

---

15 Reference is to Genesis, Chapter 39. Five more biblical allusions follow in Melchior's speech: two from Genesis, Chapter 19, one from Chapter 38. Abishag will be found in I Kings 1, Vashti in the apocryphal book of Esther, Chapter 1. Obviously all the boys have a secondary school background— which is also clear from their cry of : Summa cum laude!

HELMUTH: Look! —Now! —O God, O God...

ALL: Summa cum laude! Summa cum laude!

RUPRECHT: [*Taking the coin.*] Thank you very much.

HELMUTH: Give it here, you bastard.[16]

RUPRECHT: You pig!

HELMUTH: You jailbird!

RUPRECHT: [*Strikes him in the face.*] There!

[*He runs away.*]

HELMUTH: [*Running after him.*] I'll kill him!

THE REST: [*On their trail.*] After him! Give it to him! Get going! Get going!

MELCHIOR: [*Alone, turning toward the window.*] —That's where the lightning conductor comes down. —You have to wrap a handkerchief around it. —When I think of *her*, the blood rushes to my head. And Moritz—It's as if I had lead in my shoes. —I'll go to a newspaper office. "Pay me by the hundred, I'll sell papers—collect news—write—local stuff— ethical questions—psycho-physical..." It's not so easy to starve any more. Luncheonettes, temperance cafés. —The building is sixty feet high and the stucco's coming off... She hates me—she hates me because I took her freedom away. Whatever I do about it now, it remains rape. —I can only hope, gradually, over the years... In one week's time it's a new moon. Tomorrow I'll grease the hinges. By Saturday I must somehow find out who has the key. —Sunday evening, during the service, a cataleptic fit—God grant no one else falls sick! —It all stretches out before me as if it had already

---

16 The boys masturbate. The aim is to ejaculate and hit the coin with the sperm. Ruprecht claims to have hit it first but Helmuth disputes the claim.

happened. I can get over the window sill without trouble—swing—hold—but you have to wrap a handkerchief round it. —Here comes the Grand Inquisitor.

[*Exit left. Enter* DR. PROCRUSTES *at right with a* LOCKSMITH.]

DR. PROCRUSTES: . . . I know the windows are on the fourth floor and that nettles have been planted underneath. But do degenerates care about nettles? —Last winter one climbed out of a skylight on us, and we had all the trouble of picking him up, carting him off, interring him . . .

THE LOCKSMITH: Do you want the grating of wrought iron?

DR. PROCRUSTES: Wrought iron, yes. And, since it can't be set in, riveted.

SCENE 5

A bedroom. —MRS. BERGMANN, INA MÜLLER, *and* DR. FIZZPOWDER. —WENDLA *in bed.*

DR. FIZZPOWDER: How old are you actually?

WENDLA: Fourteen and a half.

DR. FIZZPOWDER: I've been prescribing Blaud's pills for fifteen years, and in a large number of cases I've had the most striking successes. I prefer them to cod-liver oil or iron tonics. Begin with three or four pills a day and increase the dose as rapidly as you can stand it. In the case of Fräulein Elfriede Baroness von Witzleben I ordered the dose increased by one pill every three days. The baroness misunderstood me and increased the dose by three pills every day. After scarcely three weeks she was able to accompany her mama to Bad Pyrmont for an after-cure. From tiring walks and extra meals I shall excuse you. In return for which, my dear child, you must be all the more diligent in taking exercise, and you must ask for food as soon as your appetite returns. Soon thereafter the palpitations will cease, not to mention the headaches, shivering, giddiness—and these terrible digestive disturbances of yours. Eight days after the cure began, Fräulein Elfriede Baroness von Witzleben ate a whole roast chicken garnished with potatoes in their jackets—for breakfast.

MRS. BERGMANN: May I offer you a glass of wine, Herr Doktor?

DR. FIZZPOWDER: Thank you, my dear Mrs. Bergmann. My carriage is waiting. Don't take it to heart. In a few weeks our little patient will be as fresh and lively as a gazelle. So take comfort! —Good day, Mrs. Bergmann. Good day, dear child. Good day, ladies. Good day!

[MRS. BERGMANN *escorts him to the door.*]

INA: [*At the window.*] —Your plane tree is changing color again already. —Can you see it from your bed? A short-lived splendor, hardly worth the joy we feel to see it come and go. —I must be going soon too. Müller'll be waiting for me outside the post office, and I have to go to the dressmaker first. Mucki is getting his first pair of trousers, and Karl's going to have a new woolen suit for the winter.

WENDLA: Sometimes I feel so happy—all joy and sunshine. I never dreamt one's heart could be light. I want to go out and walk in the meadows in the evening sun, look for primroses by the river, sit down on the bank and dream . . . And then I get the toothache and feel I must be going to die. I go hot and cold, it gets black in front of my eyes, and the monster flies in again. —Every time I wake up I see Mother crying. Oh, that hurts so much—I can't tell you, Ina!

INA: —Shall I put your pillow a little higher for you?

MRS. BERGMANN: [*Coming back.*] He thinks the vomiting will die down, and then it will be all right to get up again . . . I think it would be better for you to get up soon, too, Wendla.

INA: The next time I drop in, you'll be bouncing about the house again, I'm sure. —Good-by, Mother. I simply must go to the dressmaker's. God bless you, Wendla, dear. [*Kissing her.*] Get better quickly!

WENDLA: Good-by, Ina. —Bring me some primroses when you come again. Good-by! Give my love to the boys.

[*Exit* INA.]

WENDLA: [*Cont'd.*] What did he say when he was outside, Mother?

MRS. BERGMANN: He didn't say anything. —He said Baroness von Witzleben had a tendency to faint, too. He said it was usual with anemia.

WENDLA: Did he say I had anemia, Mother?

MRS. BERGMANN: You're to drink milk and eat meat and vegetables as soon as your appetite comes back.

WENDLA: Mother, I don't think I have anemia . . .

MRS. BERGMANN: You have anemia!

WENDLA: No, Mother. I know it, I feel it, it's not anemia, it's dropsy . . .

MRS. BERGMANN: Didn't he say you had anemia? Calm yourself, child. You'll get better.

WENDLA: No, I've got dropsy. Oh, Mother, I'm going to die!

MRS. BERGMANN: You're not going to die, child . . . Merciful Heavens!

WENDLA: Then why do you cry so terribly?

MRS. BERGMANN: It's not dropsy! You're going to have a baby, Wendla! A baby! Why have you done this to me?

WENDLA: —I haven't done anything to you. —

MRS. BERGMANN: On top of all, don't deny it, Wendla—I know everything, I just didn't have it in me to speak about it. — Wendla, my Wendla...!

WENDLA: But it's impossible, Mother: I'm not married.

MRS. BERGMANN: Great God above—that's just it, you're not married. That's the dreadful thing! —Wendla, Wendla, Wendla, what have you done?

WENDLA: I don't know, Heaven knows I don't know. We were in the hay... I never loved anyone but you, Mother, you!

MRS. BERGMANN: My precious—

WENDLA: Why didn't you tell me everything, Mother?

MRS. BERGMANN: Child, child, pull yourself together. Don't despair! How could I tell such things to a fourteen-year-old girl? It'd have been the end of the world. I've treated you no different than my mother treated me. —Let's place our trust in God, Wendla, let's hope for mercy, and do our part... Why are you trembling, Wendla?

WENDLA: Someone's at the door.

MRS. BERGMANN: I didn't hear anything, dear.

[*Goes to the door and opens it.*]

WENDLA: I did. Very clearly. —Who can it be?

MRS. BERGMANN: —No one—Schmidt's mother, from Garden Street. —You've come at the right time, Mother Schmidt.

SCENE 6

VINTAGERS—men and women alike[17]—in the vineyard. —In the west the sun is sinking behind the mountain peaks. The clear sound of bells from the valley below. HÄNSCHEN RILOW *and* ERNST RÖBEL, *at the uppermost vine trellis, beneath the overhanging cliffs, rolling in the drying grass.*

ERNST: —I've been overdoing it.

HÄNSCHEN: Let's not be sad. —Pity, the time flies.

ERNST: You see them hanging there and can't do anything about it. And tomorrow they're in the wine press.

HÄNSCHEN: I find hunger unbearable, but fatigue is just as bad!

ERNST: I can't manage any more.

HÄNSCHEN: Just this one shining muscatel!

ERNST: I can stretch my stomach just so much.

HÄNSCHEN: When I bend the spray, it swings from my mouth to yours. Neither of us need move—just bite the grapes off and let the stalk spring back to the vine.

ERNST: You make a good resolution. "But lo! the strength that fled is renewed again."

HÄNSCHEN: Add the flaming firmament—and the evening bells—I don't ask much more of the future.

ERNST: I sometimes see myself as already a worthy pastor with a good-natured homebody for a wife, a voluminous library,

---

17 Here Wedekind's stage direction would seem to call for a "cast of thousands." Or perhaps at this point he had in mind a "book drama" (his own term), wherein a crowd of vintagers would exist only in the mind's eye. More important: this scene, however staged, or left unstaged, is in a special mode, which critics will handle by citing dream sequences or by invoking such entities as "Expressionism."

and duties to perform—positions to hold—in every sphere of society. Six days for meditation; on the seventh, one opens one's mouth. When you take your walk, schoolboys and girls shake hands with you. And when you return home, the coffee is steaming, a big cake is served, and girls bring apples in through the garden door. —Can you imagine anything finer?

HÄNSCHEN: What *I* imagine is half-closed eyelashes, half-opened lips, and Turkish draperies! —Look, I don't believe in their grand manner: our elders pull their long faces to hide their stupidities from us. Among themselves they call each other dunderheads just like us. —When I'm a millionaire, I'll build a monument to God. —Think of the future as a bowl of milk with sugar and cinnamon on it. One man knocks it over and bawls, another churns it up and sweats. Why not skim it? Or don't you believe one can learn to?

ERNST: —Let's skim it!

HÄNSCHEN: And leave what's left for the hens. —I've got my head out of many a noose before . . .

ERNST: Let's skim it, Hänschen! —How can you laugh?

HÄNSCHEN: Are you starting over?[18]

ERNST: Somebody has to start.

HÄNSCHEN: When we think back in thirty years to an evening like this maybe it will seem indescribably beautiful.

ERNST: How does it get this way—all by itself?

HÄNSCHEN: Why shouldn't it?

18 Sex in this scene is presented obliquely and sometimes symbolically, as in the long stage direction at the outset and the talk of *grapes* swinging "from my mouth to yours." It seems that orgasm was reached just before the scene opens and will be reached again just after it closes, now that the boys' strength ". . . is renewed again" and they "start over." Priapus is the god of vineyards.

ERNST: If one were alone—one might burst out crying.

HÄNSCHEN: Let's not be sad!

[*He kisses him on the mouth.*]

ERNST: [*Kisses him.*] I left the house thinking I'd just speak to you and go right back.

HÄNSCHEN: I was waiting for you. —Virtue's not a bad suit of clothes, but you need quite a figure to fill it.

ERNST: It hangs pretty loose on *us*. —I wouldn't have known contentment if I hadn't met you. —I love you, Hänschen, as I have never loved a living soul . . .

HÄNSCHEN: Let's not be sad. —When we think back in thirty years, we'll make a joke of it. —And it's all so beautiful now. The mountains glow, grapes hang down into our mouths, and the evening wind caresses the cliffs like a playful little flirt . . .

SCENE 7

A clear November night. Dry leaves rustle on bushes and trees. Ragged clouds race across the moon. —MELCHIOR *climbs over the graveyard wall.*

MELCHIOR: [*Jumping down inside the wall.*] The wolves won't follow me here. —While they're searching the brothels I can catch my breath and see how I'm doing . . . My coat's in rags, my pockets are empty, just about everything is a threat to me . . . I must try to push on through the woods by day . . . I've stepped on a cross. —The flowers would have frozen anyhow. The ground is bare all around. —In the kingdom of the dead!

Climbing through that skylight wasn't as hard as the journey: this was the one thing I was unprepared for.

I'm suspended over the abyss—the ground has fallen away beneath my feet, it's faded clear away. —I wish I'd stayed there!

Why must it be she? —Why not the one who was to blame? —Inscrutable Providence! —I would have broken stones and starved...!

What keeps me going? —Crime follows crime. Deeper and deeper in the mire. Not even the strength left to put an end to it...

I wasn't bad! —I wasn't bad! —I wasn't bad...

No mortal ever wandered among graves so full of envy— Pah—I wouldn't have the courage! Oh, if only madness would overtake me—this very night!

I must look over there among the recent ones. —The wind whistles a different note against every stone—a symphony of distress. —The decaying wreaths are torn in two. They dangle in pieces by their long ribbons around the marble crosses—a forest of scarecrows. Scarecrows on every grave. Each more horrible than the last. Tall as houses. The very devils run from them. —How coldly the gilt letters glitter! ...The weeping willow groans and runs over the inscription with giant fingers...

A praying cherub—A tablet—

A cloud casts its shadow on the earth—how it rushes and howls—it is massing in the east like an army on the march. —Not a star in the sky.

—Evergreen around that little plot. Evergreen? — Wendla...

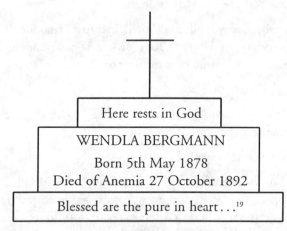

Here rests in God

WENDLA BERGMANN
Born 5th May 1878
Died of Anemia 27 October 1892

Blessed are the pure in heart...[19]

MELCHIOR: [*Cont'd.*] And I am her murderer. —I am her murderer! —Nothing is left but despair. —I mustn't cry here. I must get away—away—

MORITZ STIEFEL: [*Comes stomping over the graves, his head under his arm.*] One moment, Melchior. This opportunity will not be repeated in a hurry. You've no idea how everything is bound up with time and place...

MELCHIOR: Where have *you* come from?

MORITZ: By the wall there. You knocked my cross over. I lie by the wall. —Give me your hand, Melchior...

---

19 This is how the German editions, presumably following Wedekind's MS., have presented these lines. As no audience could be expected to read such an inscription, we must imagine either that Melchior reads it aloud or that (in a highly expressionistic production) the inscription is suddenly made legible to the public by enlargement and projection. Another oddity is the date of Wendla's death in view of the fact that Wedekind says he wrote the play "Autumn 1890 to Easter 1891." The biblical quotation ends with "...for they shall see God" (Matthew 5.8). With this "quote" the community would cover up Wendla's sin and/or victimization, the irony being that she really was (in a sense unknown to them) pure in heart.

MELCHIOR: You are *not* Moritz Stiefel!

MORITZ: Give me your hand. You'll live to thank me. Things aren't going to be easy for you. It is a strangely lucky encounter. —I came over on purpose....

MELCHIOR: Don't you sleep, then?

MORITZ: Not what you people call sleeping. —We sit on church steeples and rooftops...anywhere...

MELCHIOR: Without rest?

MORITZ: For the fun of it. —We haunt Maypoles and solitary forest shrines. —We hover over crowds, gardens, public fairgrounds, places where disasters happen. —Indoors, we cower in the chimney corner or behind the bed curtains. —Give me your hand. —We have no truck with each other, but we see and hear all that goes on in the world. We know that what men do and strive for is folly, and we laugh about it.

MELCHIOR: What good does that do?

MORITZ: What good does it have to do? —We can't be got at— not by anything—not by good, not by bad. We are 'way high above all earthly goings-on, each for himself alone. We have nothing to do with each other. Interaction would be boring. We none of us still cherish anything that we might lose later. We are above the battle—both the weeping and the laughter. We are satisfied with ourselves. —The living we despise unspeakably, we can hardly even pity them. Their doings cheer us up. Being alive, they are not really to be pitied. We smile at their tragedies, each of us for himself, and make our observations on the subject. —Give me your hand. If you give me your hand, you'll fall down laughing at the emotion with which you give me your hand.

MELCHIOR: Doesn't that disgust you?

MORITZ: We're above such disgust. We smile. —I was among the mourners at my funeral. A most entertaining experience! That's what being above it all means, Melchior. I bawled with the best of them, and then slipped over to the cemetery wall to hold my sides laughing. Only by being above it all like us are you in a position to swallow all the hogwash... There must have been quite a bit of laughter at *my* expense before I soared aloft.

MELCHIOR: I have no wish to laugh at myself.

MORITZ: ... The living are truly not to be pitied. —I admit this would never have occurred to *me* either, but now it's inconceivable to me that men can be so naïve. I've seen through the whole swindle. Not the smallest cloud remains. —How can you hesitate, Melchior? Give me your hand. Before you can turn round, you'll be sky-high above yourself. —Your life is a sin of omission.

MELCHIOR: —Can you forget, you people?

MORITZ: We can do anything. —Give me your hand. —We can deplore youth that takes its timidity for idealism and age that dies of a broken heart rather than surrender its superiority. We see emperors tremble at a street ballad, and beggars at the mention of the last trump. We look through the actor's mask and watch the poet putting his mask on in the dark. We see that this man is contented in his beggary. In the weary and heavy-laden we descry the capitalist. We observe lovers and see that they blush before each other, they sense that they are deceived deceivers. We see parents bringing children into the world in order to shout at them: "How lucky you are to have such parents!" and we see the children go and do likewise. We can eavesdrop on the innocent in their love-starved loneliness, on the two-bit whore reading Schiller... We see God and the Devil trying to put each other out of countenance, and in our hearts we realize that they're both drunk... This is peace, Melchior, contentment. —You need only offer me your little finger. —Your hair may be white as snow before another such opportunity presents itself.

MELCHIOR: If I agree, Moritz, it will be from self-contempt. I see myself as a pariah. All that gave me courage is in the grave. Nothing now, as I see it, stands between me and doom. To myself I am the most execrable creature alive.

MORITZ: Then, why hesitate?

[*Enter a* MAN IN A MASK.]

THE MAN IN THE MASK: [*To* MELCHIOR.] You're trembling with hunger. You're in no position to judge. [*To* MORITZ.] Go away!

MELCHIOR: Who are you?

THE MAN IN THE MASK: That will become clear. [*To* MORITZ.] Get going! —What do you think *you're* doing here? —Why don't you have your head on?

MORITZ: I shot myself.

THE MAN IN THE MASK: Then stay where you belong. Your time is past. Don't molest us with the stench of your grave. How can you? Just look at your fingers. Pah! They're crumbling already.

MORITZ: Please don't send me away...

MELCHIOR: Who are *you*, sir?

MORITZ: Don't send me away. Please! Let me join you for a while. I won't cross you in any way. —It's so gruesome down below.

THE MAN IN THE MASK: Then why do you prate about being above it all? —You know quite well that's all humbug—sour grapes. Why do you lie so assiduously, you bogy? —Well, if it's such a priceless boon, stay for all I care. But refrain from empty boasting, my friend —and please leave your dead hand out of the game.

MELCHIOR: Are you going to tell me who you are, or not?

THE MAN IN THE MASK: Not. —I suggest that you place yourself in my hands. I would give your survival my best attention.

MELCHIOR: You are —my father?

THE MAN IN THE MASK: Wouldn't you know your father by his voice?

MELCHIOR: No.

THE MAN IN THE MASK: —At the moment your father is seeking solace in the doughty arms of your mother. —I will unlock the world to you. Your loss of equilibrium arises from the misery of your present position. With a warm dinner in your belly you'll laugh at it.

MELCHIOR: [Aside.] They can't both be the devil. [Aloud.] After what I am guilty of, a warm dinner cannot give me back my peace of mind.

THE MAN IN THE MASK: That depends on the dinner! —I can tell you this much: that little girl would have given birth splendidly. She was superbly built. It was Mother Schmidt's abortion pills that did for her. —I will take you among men. I will give you the opportunity to enlarge your horizon in the most amazing way. I will acquaint you, without exception, with everything of interest that the world has to offer.

MELCHIOR: Who *are* you? Who *are* you? —I can't entrust myself to a man I don't know.

THE MAN IN THE MASK: You can't get to know me unless you entrust yourself to me.

MELCHIOR: You think so?

THE MAN IN THE MASK: It *is* so. —Anyhow, you have no choice.

MELCHIOR: At any moment I can give my friend here my hand.

THE MAN IN THE MASK: Your friend is a charlatan. "We are above the battle, we smile." Put a penny in a man's pocket, and he'll stop smiling. Your humorist friend is the most pitiful creature in all creation. And the most deplorable.

MELCHIOR: Whatever *he* may be, tell me who *you* are or I give this humorist my hand.

THE MAN IN THE MASK: Well?

MORITZ: He's right, Melchior. I was bragging. Accept his guidance. Make use of him. If he's masked, he's masked, you know where you are with him.

MELCHIOR: Do you believe in God?

THE MAN IN THE MASK: It all depends.

MELCHIOR: Who invented gunpowder?

THE MAN IN THE MASK: Berthold Schwarz—alias Konstatin Anklitzen, a Franciscan monk, about 1330, at Freiburg im Breisgau.

MORITZ: If only he hadn't!

THE MAN IN THE MASK: Then you'd have hanged yourself.

MELCHIOR: Where do you stand on morality?

THE MAN IN THE MASK: Fellow! —Am I some little pupil of yours?

MELCHIOR: And if you're not?

MORITZ: —Please don't quarrel. What good does it do? —What's the point of our sitting together, two alive and one dead, here in the churchyard at two o'clock in the morning, if we're going to quarrel like a bunch of drunks? —It should be a pleasure to me to be present at these negotiations. —If you want to quarrel, I'll put my head under my arm and go.

MELCHIOR: Still the same timid old Moritz!

THE MAN IN THE MASK: The ghost is not wrong. One should not leave one's dignity out of account. —I take our morality to be the real product of two imaginary factors. The imaginary factors are "I ought to" and "I want to."[20] The product is called "morality." Its reality is undeniable.

MORITZ: If only you'd told me that before! —My morality drove me to my death. I took up the murderous weapon for my parents' sake. "Honor they mother and thy father and thy days may be long." In any case, the old saying has been made to look rather silly.

THE MAN IN THE MASK: Don't permit yourself illusions, my friend! Your parents would no more have died of it than you need have. Strictly considered, they would have raged and thundered solely from physical need.

MELCHIOR: That may be true as far as it goes. —But I can assure you, sir, that if I'd gone ahead and given Moritz my hand just now, it's my morality that would have been responsible.

THE MAN IN THE MASK: But you didn't. Because you're not Moritz.

MORITZ: Is the difference so essential? You might have happened on me too, Stranger, as I trudged through the alder plantations with that pistol in my pocket.

THE MAN IN THE MASK: Then you don't remember me? Even at the last moment you were hesitating between death and… life. But this is hardly the place to prolong so searching a debate.

20 The formulation was no doubt suggested by Goethe's essay, "Shakespeare und kein Ende." Which to some will mean that the Masked Man is Goethe. And, to be sure, the play was dedicated to the Masked Man by Wedekind, the Goethe worshipper.

MORITZ: It's certainly getting cold, gentlemen. —They may have dressed me in my Sunday suit, but I'm wearing neither shirt nor shorts.

MELCHIOR: Farewell, dear Moritz. Where this man is taking me I don't know. But he *is* a man...

MORITZ: I tried to kill you, Melchior, but don't hold it against me. Put it down to lingering affection. —I'd gladly moan and groan for the rest of my life if I could go out with you one more time.

THE MAN IN THE MASK: To each his own: to you the soothing consciousness that you have *nothing*, to you the enervating doubts about *everything*. —Farewell.

MELCHIOR: Farewell, Moritz! Thank you for coming. How many untroubled, happy days we've had in the fourteen years! In the years ahead, things may go well with me or badly, I may become a different man ten times over, but, come what may, I shall never forget *you*.

MORITZ: Thanks, thanks, dear heart.

MELCHIOR: Though I live to be an old man with white hair, you may still be closer to me, Moritz, than all the living.

MORITZ: Thank you. —Good luck on your journey, gentlemen. — Don't let me keep you.

THE MAN IN THE MASK: Come, my boy.

[*He puts his arm in* MELCHIOR*'s and withdraws him over the graves.*]

MORITZ: [*Alone.*] —So here I sit with my head on my arm. —The moon hides her face, unveils herself again, and looks not a bit the smarter. —So I shall go back to my little plot, set up my cross which that madcap trampled down, and, when everything is in order, I shall lie on my back again, warm myself with the putrefaction, and smile...

THE LIFE OF THE DRAMA

by ERIC BENTLEY

"The most adventurous critic in America."

—Kenneth Tynan

"Eric Bentley's radical new look at the grammar of theatre...is a work of exceptional virtue, and readers who find more in it to disagree with than I do will still, I think, want to call it CENTRAL, IN-DISPENSABLE...If you see any crucial interest in such topics as the death of Cordelia, Godot's non-arrival...THIS IS A BOOK TO BE READ AGAIN AND AGAIN."

—Frank Kermode, *The New York Review of Books*

"*The Life Of The Drama*...is a remarkable exploration of the roots and bases of dramatic art, THE MOST FAR REACHING AND REVELATORY WE HAVE HAD."

—Richard Gilman, *Book Week*

ISBN: 1-55783-110-6

APPLAUSE